BETHLEHEM
CAROLS UNPACKED

Creative ideas for Christmas carol services

Lucy Moore and Martyn Payne
with Bible*Lands*

ACKNOWLEDGMENTS

The material in this book has been compiled by the Barnabas ministry team in consultation with Bible*Lands*, who have provided the stories of the work that they support in the lands of the Bible. The inspiration for the book is Bible*Lands*' *Bethlehem Carol Sheet*, which features children who have been helped by projects run by Bible*Lands* Partners.

Barnabas

Working in partnership with Lucy Moore and Martyn Payne, additional material has been contributed by Sue Doggett, Commissioning Editor, Barnabas, and Alison Harris, who was a member of the Barnabas team until she commenced training for ordination at the Queen's Foundation, Birmingham, in September 2007.

With thanks to Margaret Withers for providing invaluable advice and input to the sections concerning the carols and Christmas hymns and for her support in reading and commenting on the manuscript.

Bible*Lands*

Additional material has been contributed by Alison MacTier, Communications Resources Manager for Bible*Lands*. Alison joined Bible*Lands* in 2003 and has overall responsibility for the charity's publications. She previously spent twelve years in commercial book publishing, where she worked as an editor in both children's and educational books and was Editorial Manager for five years. Alison has also worked as Commissioning Editor on a number of RE titles.

With thanks to Nigel Edward-Few, Director of Bible*Lands*, and his staff team for their invaluable support and advice.

Lucy Moore has been part of the Barnabas team since 2001. With a special interest in drama and storytelling, all-age church and collective worship in schools, her work takes her into schools and churches across the UK. She is an accredited Godly Play teacher, and is part of the Children's Advisory Group for Portsmouth Diocese, on the leadership team of Messy Church and an Associate Missioner for Fresh Expressions. Lucy enjoys both performance work and helping all those working in schools and churches to explore creative and appropriate ways of opening up the Bible with children.

Her published work includes *The Gospels Unplugged*, *Topsy Turvy Christmas*, *The Lord's Prayer Unplugged*, and *Messy Church*, all published by Barnabas.

Martyn Payne joined the Barnabas team in January 2003, having worked with CMS as National Children's Work Coordinator for several years. Martyn has wide experience of working with schools and churches to explore ways of opening up the Bible with children.

Before his time with CMS, Martyn worked for 18 years as a teacher in East London, leading a modern languages department and being involved in the planning, writing and delivery of RE lessons.

Martyn is an experienced workshop leader, Godly Play teacher and speaker and has collaborated with children's advisers and education officers in major school, church and family events across the UK. Based in London, he is available to lead RE days in schools, INSET training, church-based training sessions and workshops, and to help run special events throughout the UK. Martyn is author of *A-cross the World* and *Footsteps to the Feast*, both published by Barnabas.

Text copyright © Lucy Moore and Martyn Payne 2008
The authors assert the moral right
to be identified as the authors of this work

Published by
The Bible Reading Fellowship
15 The Chambers, Vineyard
Abingdon OX14 3FE
United Kingdom
Tel: +44 (0)1865 319700
Email: enquiries@brf.org.uk
Website: www.brf.org.uk

ISBN 978 1 84101 534 7
First published 2008
10 9 8 7 6 5 4 3 2 1 0

Acknowledgments
Unless otherwise stated, scripture quotations are taken from the Contemporary English Version
of the Bible published by HarperCollins Publishers, copyright © 1991, 1992, 1995 American
Bible Society.

Unless otherwise stated, scripture quotations are taken from The New Revised Standard
Version of the Bible, Anglicized Edition, copyright © 1989, 1995 by the Division of Christian
Education of the National Council of the Churches of Christ in the USA, and are used by
permission. All rights reserved.

Scripture quotations taken from the Holy Bible, New International Version, copyright © 1973,
1978, 1984 by International Bible Society, are used by permission of Hodder & Stoughton
Publishers, a division of Hodder Headline Ltd. All rights reserved. 'NIV' is a registered
trademark of International Bible Society. UK trademark number 1448790.

Scriptures quoted from the Good News Bible published by The Bible Societies/HarperCollins
Publishers Ltd, UK © American Bible Society 1966, 1971, 1976, 1992, used with permission.

'Christmas poor' by David Adam, from *The Edge of Glory: Prayers in the Celtic Tradition* (Triangle,
1985), reprinted by permission of SPCK.

Extract from *Some Other Rainbow* by John McCarthy and Jill Morrell (Bantam, 1993), reprinted
by permission of the Random House Group Ltd.

Performance and copyright
The right to perform *Bethlehem Carols Unpacked* drama material is included in the purchase
price, so long as the performance is in an amateur context, for instance in church services,
schools or holiday club venues. Where any charge is made to audiences, written permission
must be obtained from the author, who can be contacted through the publishers. A fee or
royalties may be payable for the right to perform the script in that context.

A catalogue record for this book is available from the British Library

Printed in Singapore by Craft Print International Ltd

✳

Preface

ABOUT BIBLE*LANDS*

Bible*Lands* has been at the heart of a Christian compassionate ministry for more than 150 years. It began in 1854 at the height of the Crimean War. Throughout the second half of the 19th, the 20th and now into the 21st century, Bible*Lands* has maintained its crucial focus: its mission remains to serve the poor, vulnerable and disadvantaged in the lands of the Bible, regardless of their faith or nationality.

As a non-governmental Christian agency, Bible*Lands*' vision is to enable and resource local Christians to respond strategically and effectively to the changing needs of the region and its people through education, health and community development.

It works in partnership with more than 50 projects in Israel and the Occupied Territories, Lebanon and Egypt.

ISRAEL AND THE OCCUPIED TERRITORIES

In Israel and the Occupied Territories, the birthplace of the Christian faith, Bible*Lands* Partners work in some of the most challenging conditions imaginable. The communities whom they serve endure the daily consequences of occupation—poverty, unemployment, a lack of social cohesion, disruption to services and education, economic uncertainty and a shortage of basic commodities, curfews and travel restrictions. Despite these underlying conditions, Bible*Lands*' Project Partners strive to maintain continuity and stability in their communities, particularly for the sake of the many children in their care.

EGYPT

In Egypt, Bible*Lands*' Project Partners provide urgent medical and social care to the people of a country where one third of the population live either very close to or under the poverty line. In a population of 75 million, the geography of the land means that the majority live in vastly overcrowded cities, all fighting for survival, while those living in rural areas face unimaginable poverty, disease and deprived living conditions. Several of Bible*Lands*' Project Partners, in Cairo particularly, also provide much-needed care to thousands of refugees who arrive in Egypt having fled from Sudan, Somalia and Ethiopia, many having lost everything.

LEBANON

In Lebanon, after the terrible destruction of civil conflict and almost continuous regional warfare from the 1967 war right up to the present time, the economy has become crippled by debt and prospects for recovery are bleak. In a country where an increasing number face unemployment and great hardship, as well as fears for an uncertain future, Bible*Lands*' Project Partners continue to offer hope. They help to provide many of the key services that the state cannot afford to provide.

Bible*Lands*' 50 Partner Projects in these three countries work in three key areas of service:

- **Education:** Bible*Lands* supports schools and colleges that offer education to the highest standards for children whose families cannot afford it. It also supports many vocational training programmes across all three countries for able-bodied and disabled people, including a degree-level nurse training scheme. Special education programmes are provided for those with special educational needs and learning difficulties.

- **Health:** Bible*Lands* funds hospitals, clinics and local primary health care centres. It also supports projects that offer special needs care and support, and education and rehabilitation both for those who have been seriously injured or suffered major trauma and for those with congenital physical and mental disabilities.
- **Community development:** Bible*Lands* provides social care to children who have lost one or both parents and those in particularly deprived circumstances, local infrastructure support, revolving loans, education and technical support to communities, housing, primary health care, literacy programmes, and support and care for refugees.

Bible*Lands* is funded entirely through generous donations, sponsorship schemes, appeals, legacies and grants from individuals, churches and a limited number of trusts.

Without this prayerful and financial ministry and the encouragement of its supporters and donors, the valuable work of helping so many in need could not continue. In such an unsettled region, this support has never been as vital as it is now.

The enduring popularity of the *Bethlehem Carol Sheet* for more than 55 years has been one way in which, at Christmas time, Bible*Lands* and its Project Partners are able to share in prayer and worship with their supporters and raise funds across the UK and beyond for this valuable work.

This creative book provides an excellent opportunity to extend the nature of this celebration in a new and contemporary way. It brings the Christmas story to life in the 21st-century Holy Land, by including powerful stories about the work that Bible*Lands* currently supports in the region where the Christmas story first began. We hope and believe that these stories will interest and inspire all those taking part in a carol service.

There are many ways in which you can offer your continued support throughout the year. If you would like further information about how you can become involved in this work, Bible*Lands* would love to hear from you at: Bible*Lands*, PO Box 50, High Wycombe, Bucks HP15 7QU. More information on Bible*Lands* can also be found at: www.biblelands.org.uk.

CONTENTS

Part Three: Using a Bible*Lands* project related to the carols

Part Four: Involving children in a creative carol service

FOREWORD

The first years of the 21st century have witnessed a growing interest and participation in Christmas carol services. In a world increasingly reliant on virtual experience and remote communication, it seems that our appetite to gather together, to stand and sit and listen and sing, is undimmed. For any of us who plan these services, the challenges are considerable. We are charged with bringing to life the greatest story ever told, in words ancient and contemporary, music traditional and modern.

This interesting, creative and inspiring book helps us to navigate our passage through the cultural filters on the way from first-century Palestine through medieval Europe to the modern-day United Kingdom and back to the contemporary Holy Lands. In these pages we will hear once again the familiar songs and stories; we will also sharpen our Christmas faith on the anvil of profound suffering and conflict. Bible*Lands* overseas partners tell their stories with compelling simplicity and a moving faith that shakes us out of our complacency and causes us ever more fervently to 'pray for the peace of Jerusalem' and her neighbours.

We have a duty, as leaders of worship, to offer familiarity in a Christmas celebration that, for many, is a touchstone in an ever-changing society. But we also have a duty to evoke, in contemporary language and visual communication, the awesome reality of the incarnation. We are bound to proclaim the God who knows no boundaries of space or time but who comes to earth and knows our human life. These remarkable stories and tunes give us a new language to say again that God is with us in the vulnerability of a baby, and with the light and power of his Son.

Canon Lucy Winkett, Precentor of St Paul's Cathedral

*

INTRODUCTION

CAROLS AND CAROL SINGING: A BRIEF HISTORY

A carol is a joyful religious song created and sung by ordinary people. The root meaning of the word 'carol' is 'to dance in a ring' and probably came from the Old French *caroller*, through the Latin *choraula* and, originally, the Greek *choros*, which was a circling dance. Traditional carols are essentially joyful. Even when the subject is solemn, the music is lively and the words trip easily off the tongue.

Carols first became popular in the 15th century as earlier restrictions on music and drama in church decreased. Some carols had pagan roots but were adapted to the Christian faith, along with other customs. Their subjects are down-to-earth and include references to plants and animals, food and drink. 'The holly and the ivy' and 'Here we come a wassailing' are popular examples of carols in which a Christian dimension has been added to these subjects. The church sang Gregorian chant in Latin, while the people sang and danced to carols in the street, the home and the inn.

Most carols that have survived are connected with Advent and Christmas, but there are also carols to be sung at Easter, on saints' days and at different seasons of the year. The style varies: many have skipping rhythms, some have choruses and others are narratives in the style of ballads. All Christian nations have carols; those of France are called *Noels*, a word that probably came into English as 'Nowell' through the Normans. The origins of this word are discussed in more detail in the chapter on 'The first Nowell'.

In the 17th century, when the Puritans disapproved of celebrating religious feasts, including Christmas, and dancing was banned, carol singing declined and was almost forgotten. In 1871, however, *Christmas Carols New and Old* by Revd H.R. Bramley and Dr John

Stainer was published and brought 13 traditional carols and some original compositions into wide and popular use. The effect of this book was enormous. Some of the arrangements were weak and rather pious but the restoration of the traditional carol is largely owed to them. It was gradually recognized that, with the advent of universal education and wider travel, the great wealth of folk music, including carols, was in danger of being lost. Composers including Ralph Vaughan Williams collected and published many traditional words and melodies in the *English Hymnal* (1906) and the *Oxford Book of Carols* (1928).

The last 70 years has shown a continuous increase in carol services, along with Festivals of Nine Lessons and Carols, first devised in Truro Cathedral and later popularized by annual broadcasts from King's College, Cambridge. For example, the service records of Gloucester Cathedral record no carol services before 1930, but by 1990 a carol service was being held almost every evening during the fortnight before Christmas. Today, carol services are held in almost every church and school as well as numerous concert halls. New arrangements of carols are published every year, and seasonal CDs are increasingly popular.

The *Bethlehem Carol Sheet* has done much to make carols from every part of the world available to carol singers and services. The eleven items chosen for this book cover a wide range of styles, periods and traditions. Only 'God rest you merry, gentlemen' and 'The first Nowell' are traditional carols. The others range from hymns written to teach children in Sunday school (such as 'Once in royal David's city' and 'Away in a manger') to a biblical text, 'While shepherds watched their flocks by night', which is a metrical version of Luke 2:8–14. Works by leading churchmen of their day include 'Hark! the herald-angels sing', an adaptation of words by Charles Wesley, the leading 18th-century hymn writer, set to music from Mendelssohn's oratorio *Festgesang*, and 'Good King Wenceslas' with original verses from J.M. Neale, who translated numerous early Greek and Latin hymns.

Carols were always modern in that they expressed the faith and ideas of ordinary people in their own age. Their charm lies in their being true to the culture of their time. Some of the poetry may be rough and the melodies simple, but their genuine expression of faith and life shows against sham antiquity or banality. Some comparatively modern works have kept the spirit of traditional carols in that they have been written by ordinary people for a specific purpose, often with music added by equally humble musicians. 'We three kings' and 'Silent night' are two of the best examples of modern compositions that have rightly passed into the rich heritage of carols and carol singing.

HOW TO USE THIS BOOK

Christmas is a time for remembering Jesus' own poverty and the needs of the homeless and disadvantaged. This results in an increased opportunity not only to give to national charities but also to respond to the desperate inequalities and needs of the wider world—especially in the lands where Jesus was born and carried out his ministry. Each of the well-known and well-loved carols in this book explores a particular project connected with and supported by BibleLands and, through this vehicle, the carol service can also be an ideal opening for congregations to act on these concerns through prayer and giving.

Against this background of expectations, longings and concerns, the collection in this book offers a way to blend the traditional with something new and original. Each carol includes a brief outline of the story behind its composition, together with notes on its content, meaning and biblical links. This information is intended primarily as background for those leading the carol service, but may also be useful in providing insights for an introduction to each carol, helping to place it within the framework of the service as a whole.

The eleven carols in this collection are the top eleven favourites in BibleLands' ever popular *Bethlehem Carol Sheet*, which has been produced by the charity each year since 1953. The latest edition of the carol sheet, which includes 26 of the most popular Christmas carols and hymns, is available from BibleLands. Contact details are as follows:

BibleLands
PO Box 50
High Wycombe
Buckinghamshire
HP15 7QU
Telephone: 01494 897950
Fax: 01494 897951
Email: info@biblelands.org.uk
Website: www.biblelands.org.uk

Unpacking the carols

Each of the carols (or Christmas hymns) in this book is unpacked in a variety of creative ways, including poetry, drama, material for under-fives, prayers, stories and ideas for sensory worship. The intention is to enable you to pick and mix the ideas by selecting just one of these approaches for each carol that you have chosen. For example, one carol could be introduced or followed by a short drama presentation; another might become the subject for a piece by an under-fives group; a further carol could be used to build up your nativity tableau for all ages at the front; another could be the stimulus for the prayers; a further carol could be linked to a reading and a short talk, or, as an alternative, become the inspiration for a story or piece of poetry read by older children. Finally, one carol should be reserved as the opportunity to present a creative piece about a project supported by BibleLands. Each carol in the book contains enough ideas to make this selection possible.

Bible*Lands* PowerPoint presentation material

For more information about the work of Bible*Lands*, together with a downloadable PowerPoint presentation of images relating to the projects referred to in the book, please go to www.biblelands.org.uk.

PLANNING A CAROL SERVICE

In many ways, a Christmas carol service should be one of the most straightforward acts of worship to put together each year. There is a definitive pool of readings and songs to work with and a short but powerful tradition to draw on. That legacy can become a challenge for the service planner, who dare not do anything too different, and for the congregation, who may be lulled into missing the real impact and meaning of the Christmas story through participation in something that has become overfamiliar.

One of the great opportunities presented by any carol service is that it may attract large numbers of less regular churchgoers, who are looking for that elusive mix of carols and nostalgia with which they feel comfortable (perhaps half remembered from when they were young), and may be feeling a deeper and unexpressed longing for something new to satisfy a spiritual hunger. In retelling the familiar story, there should be an opportunity for those present to grow in understanding of its eternal message while reflecting on its particular relevance in our own culture and time. Church attendance at Christmas can present a tremendous opportunity to use what is traditional to proclaim afresh the truth of the Christian faith.

Which carols should you choose? Nearly every carol is based on two short Bible passages: Luke 2:1–16 and Matthew 2:1–12. It is not easy to include all the old favourites (thus repeating the same information) while retaining a sense of movement. If you decide to use a carol that covers the whole Christmas story, this could come either at the beginning or near the end, to sum up the completed narration. The longer version of 'O come, all ye faithful' or 'The first Nowell' are well-known examples.

There are, however, those carols that focus on specific aspects of the story and these lend themselves to being used throughout the service. For example, the story of the shepherds and the angels is told in carols such as 'God rest you merry, gentlemen' and 'While shepherds watched', the scene in the stable is portrayed in 'Silent night' and 'Away in a manger', care for those in poverty is the subject of 'Good King Wenceslas', and the visit of the wise men is recorded in 'We three kings'. Reflection on the significant part that the Christmas story plays in the bigger picture of salvation is the subject of 'Once in royal David's city', 'O little town of Bethlehem' and 'Hark! the herald-angels sing'.

There is often a concern that every carol used in the service must be 'known'. However, carols need not be restricted to the most popular Christmas hymns. Many traditional carols move away from the nativity narrative and are lively and easy to sing. Not included in this book, 'I saw three ships come sailing in' and the Sussex carol 'On Christmas night, all Christians sing' are well-known examples. In the same way, the format of Bible readings and carols should not be treated as binding. Poetry, drama and dance can be effective commentaries on the story, and the use of light and movement around the building can be powerful illustrations. Furthermore, if a church has few musical facilities, an informal 'Songs of Praise' could provide the opportunity to sing popular carols while allowing time for things to be said about the carols themselves and their meaning. This format may also attract people who do not enjoy a formal or lengthy service.

For a carol service that involves young children, a maximum of five or six carols is ideal, with the service lasting not more than 40 minutes. This is especially appropriate if you plan to include a special item from a choir or introduce a new carol. It is always good practice, however, for the final hymn or carol in any service to be short and lively. People will have stood and sung for longer than usual and both the elderly and the young may feel fatigued or be ready to go home. Carols such as 'Hark! the herald-angels sing' sum up the theological message behind the Christmas story and allow the congregation to leave in a joyful frame of mind.

Each carol in the book has been given a specific subtitle that relates to the main theme of that carol, and this may be helpful in putting together a service with a particular focus, where that carol is central. You will then be able to make use of more than one creative idea from the selection given, while using other carols from the book (or elsewhere) in support.

Planning a carol service in a primary school

If you are involved in planning the carol service in a school, either as a teacher or as a member of the clergy or church team invited into the school as a guest, the ideas in this book should be helpful. The wealth of creative material available for each of the carols in the book lends itself well to special use within primary schools. One approach might be for each class to select one of the carols to explore as a class project. There is plenty of information to accompany each carol, along with the different approaches to explore it. Each class could then interpret and present their chosen carol to others. This could result in a creative carol concert at the school for friends, parents and carers or could perhaps form the basis for a service at the local church.

Worship space

Not all carol services take place in a church building, so the term 'worship space' has been used alongside references to the church as a building. The term 'worship space' denotes any space in which worship takes place, including a school hall or any other venue that is not a church building.

Involving under-fives

Much of the language and many of the theological concepts within the carols and Christmas hymns in this book are clearly beyond the understanding of very young children, but children may gain intuitively from being present in worship when these carols are sung. If young children are encouraged to feel part of the worship and appropriate ways are found to involve them, their hearts and spirits may still be touched by the experience. The activities described in the under-fives sections are designed to help young children to appreciate something of the messages and imagery contained within these popular carols, laying a foundation of positive encounter that can be built on in years to come.

Choosing which activities to use and how to organize them will depend on a number of factors related to your local situation, such as the nature of the service you are organizing, the layout of your worship space, the numbers of children involved and the availability of other adults. It is expected that young children are likely to encounter most of the carols in an all-age context where they will be accompanied by adult carers.

Sometimes it may be appropriate to put together simple activity packs that are given to each child (or their carers) as they arrive or given out at an appropriate time in the service. If you choose to do this, bear in mind that young children will probably want to do the activity as soon as they are given it, so it is worth thinking in advance of the point at which the activity would be most helpful. On other occasions, it might be more appropriate to gather groups of children at a particular time during the service to work on a creative activity. In this case, some activities may best be done while a carol is being sung, but others may best be done at an earlier part of the service so that they can be used during the singing of the carol.

Part One

THE CAROLS

AWAY IN A MANGER

Away in a manger, no crib for a bed,
The little Lord Jesus laid down his sweet head.
The stars in the bright sky looked down where he lay—
The little Lord Jesus asleep on the hay.

The cattle are lowing, the baby awakes,
But little Lord Jesus, no crying he makes.
I love thee, Lord Jesus! Look down from the sky,
And stay by my side until morning is nigh.

Be near me, Lord Jesus; I ask thee to stay
Close by me for ever, and love me, I pray.
Bless all the dear children in thy tender care,
And fit us for heaven to live with thee there.

GOD REST YOU MERRY, GENTLEMEN

God rest you merry, gentlemen,
Let nothing you dismay,
For Jesus Christ our Saviour
Was born upon this day,
To save us all from Satan's power
When we were gone astray:
    And it's tidings of comfort and joy,
    Comfort and joy,
    And it's tidings of comfort and joy.

At Bethlehem in Judah
The holy babe was born;
They laid him in a manger
On this most happy morn:
At which his mother Mary
Did neither fear nor scorn:
    And it's tidings of comfort and joy…

From God our heavenly Father
A holy angel came;
The shepherds saw the glory
And heard the voice proclaim
That Christ was born in Bethlehem
And Jesus is his name:
    And it's tidings of comfort and joy…

Continued overleaf ▶

Reproduced with permission from *Bethlehem Carols Unpacked* published by BRF 2008 (978 1 84101 534 7)
www.barnabasinchurches.org.uk

Fear not, then said the angel,
Let nothing cause you fright;
To you is born a saviour
In David's town tonight,
To free all those who trust in him
From Satan's power and might:
    And it's tidings of comfort and joy...

The shepherds at these tidings
Rejoiced in heart and mind,
And on the darkened hillside
They left their flocks behind,
And went to Bethlehem straightway
This holy child to find:
    And it's tidings of comfort and joy...

And when to Bethlehem they came
Where Christ the infant lay:
They found him in a manger
Where oxen feed on hay,
And there beside her newborn child
His mother knelt to pray:
    And it's tidings of comfort and joy...

Now to the Lord sing praises,
All people in this place!
With Christian love and fellowship
Each other now embrace,
And let this Christmas festival
All bitterness displace:
    And it's tidings of comfort and joy...

GOOD KING WENCESLAS

Good King Wenceslas look'd out
On the feast of Stephen,
When the snow lay round about,
Deep, and crisp and even;
Brightly shone the moon that night,
Though the frost was cruel,
When a poor man came in sight,
Gathering winter fuel.

'Hither page, and stand by me,
If thou know'st it telling,
Yonder peasant, who is he?
Where and what his dwelling?'
'Sire, he lives a good league hence,
Underneath the mountain,
Right against the forest fence,
By Saint Agnes' fountain.'

'Bring me flesh and bring me wine,
Bring me pine logs hither;
Thou and I will see him dine,
When we bear them thither.'
Page and monarch, forth they went,
Forth they went together,
Through the rude wind's wild lament
And the bitter weather.

Continued overleaf ▶

Reproduced with permission from *Bethlehem Carols Unpacked* published by BRF 2008 (978 1 84101 534 7)
www.barnabasinchurches.org.uk

'Sire, the night is darker now,
And the wind blows stronger;
Fails my heart, I know not how;
I can go no longer.'
'Mark my footsteps, good my page,
Tread thou in them boldly;
Thou shalt find the winter's rage
Freeze thy blood less coldly.'

In his master's steps he trod,
Where the snow lay dinted;
Heat was in the very sod
Which the saint had printed.
Therefore, Christians all, be sure,
Wealth or rank possessing,
Ye who now will bless the poor
Shall yourselves find blessing.

HARK! THE HERALD-ANGELS SING

Hark! the herald-angels sing
Glory to the newborn king,
Peace on earth and mercy mild,
God and sinners reconciled.
Joyful, all ye nations, rise,
Join the triumph of the skies;
With th' angelic host proclaim,
Christ is born in Bethlehem.
  Hark! the herald-angels sing
  Glory to the newborn king.

Christ, by highest heaven adored,
Christ, the everlasting Lord,
Late in time behold him come,
Offspring of a virgin's womb!
Veiled in flesh the Godhead see!
Hail, the incarnate deity!
Pleased as man with man to dwell,
Jesus, our Emmanuel!
  Hark! the herald-angels sing
  Glory to the newborn king.

Hail, the heaven-born Prince of Peace!
Hail, the Sun of Righteousness!
Light and life to all he brings,
Risen with healing in his wings.
Mild, he lays his glory by,
Born that we no more may die,
Born to raise the sons of earth,
Born to give them second birth.
  Hark! the herald-angels sing
  Glory to the newborn king.

Reproduced with permission from *Bethlehem Carols Unpacked* published by BRF 2008 (978 1 84101 534 7)
www.barnabasinchurches.org.uk

O COME, ALL YE FAITHFUL

O come, all ye faithful,
Joyful and triumphant,
Come ye, O come ye to Bethlehem;
Come and behold him,
Born the king of angels:
   O come, let us adore him,
   O come, let us adore him,
   O come, let us adore him,
   Christ the Lord!

God of God,
Light of light,
Lo! He abhors not the virgin's womb;
Very God,
Begotten, not created:
   O come, let us adore him…

Sing, choirs of angels,
Sing in exultation,
Sing, all ye citizens of heaven above;
Glory to God
In the highest:
   O come, let us adore him. . .

Yea, Lord, we greet thee,
Born this happy morning;
Jesus, to thee be glory given;
Word of the Father,
Now in flesh appearing:
   O come, let us adore him…

Reproduced with permission from *Bethlehem Carols Unpacked* published by BRF 2008 (978 1 84101 534 7)
www.barnabasinchurches.org.uk

O LITTLE TOWN OF BETHLEHEM

O little town of Bethlehem,
How still we see thee lie!
Above thy deep and dreamless sleep
The silent stars go by.
Yet in thy dark streets shineth
The everlasting light;
The hopes and fears of all the years
Are met in thee tonight.

O morning stars, together
Proclaim the holy birth,
And praises sing to God the king,
And peace to all on earth.
For Christ is born of Mary;
And, gathered all above,
While mortals sleep, the angels keep
Their watch of wondering love.

Continued overleaf ▶

Reproduced with permission from *Bethlehem Carols Unpacked* published by BRF 2008 (978 1 84101 534 7)
www.barnabasinchurches.org.uk

How silently, how silently,
The wondrous gift is given!
So God imparts to human hearts
The blessings of his heaven.
No ear may hear his coming;
But in this world of sin,
Where meek souls will receive him, still
The dear Christ enters in.

O holy Child of Bethlehem,
Descend to us, we pray;
Cast out our sin, and enter in,
Be born in us today.
We hear the Christmas angels
The great glad tidings tell:
O come to us, abide with us,
Our Lord Emmanuel.

ONCE IN ROYAL DAVID'S CITY

Once in royal David's city
Stood a lowly cattle-shed,
Where a mother laid her baby
In a manger for his bed.
Mary was that mother mild,
Jesus Christ her little child.

He came down to earth from heaven,
Who is God and Lord of all,
And his shelter was a stable,
And his cradle was a stall:
With the poor and mean and lowly
Lived on earth our Saviour holy.

And through all his wondrous childhood
He would honour and obey,
Love and watch the lowly maiden,
In whose gentle arms he lay.
Christian children all must be
Mild, obedient, good as he.

For he is our childhood's pattern,
Day by day like us he grew;
He was little, weak and helpless,
Tears and smiles like us he knew;
And he feeleth for our sadness,
And he shareth in our gladness.

Continued overleaf ▶

Reproduced with permission from *Bethlehem Carols Unpacked* published by BRF 2008 (978 1 84101 534 7)
www.barnabasinchurches.org.uk

And our eyes at last shall see him,
Through his own redeeming love;
For that child, so dear and gentle,
Is our Lord in heaven above;
And he leads his children on
To the place where he is gone.

Not in that poor lowly stable,
With the oxen standing by,
We shall see him, but in heaven,
Set at God's right hand on high;
When like stars his children crowned
All in white shall wait around.

SILENT NIGHT

Silent night, holy night.
All is calm, all is bright,
Round the virgin mother and child;
Holy Infant, so tender and mild,
Sleep in heavenly peace,
Sleep in heavenly peace.

Silent night, holy night.
Shepherds quail at the sight,
Glories stream from heaven afar,
Heavenly hosts sing alleluia:
Christ, the Saviour is born,
Christ, the Saviour is born.

Silent night, holy night.
Son of God, Love's pure light,
Radiant beams thy holy face,
With the dawn of redeeming grace:
Jesus, Lord, at thy birth,
Jesus, Lord, at thy birth.

Reproduced with permission from *Bethlehem Carols Unpacked* published by BRF 2008 (978 1 84101 534 7)
www.barnabasinchurches.org.uk

THE FIRST NOWELL

The first Nowell the angel did say
Was to certain poor shepherds in fields
    where they lay;
In fields where they lay, keeping their sheep,
On a cold winter's night that was so deep.
    Nowell, Nowell, Nowell, Nowell,
    Born is the king of Israel!

They lookèd up and saw a star
Shining in the East, beyond them far;
And to the earth it gave great light,
And so it continued both day and night.
    Nowell, Nowell…

And by the light of that same star,
Three wise men came from country far;
To seek for a king was their intent,
And to follow the star wherever it went.
    Nowell, Nowell…

This star drew nigh to the North-West;
O'er Bethlehem it took its rest,
And there it did both stop and stay,
Right over the place where Jesus lay.
    Nowell, Nowell…

Then entered in those wise men three,
Full reverently upon their knee,
And offered there in his presence
Their gold and myrrh and frankincense.
    Nowell, Nowell...

Then let us all with one accord
Sing praises to our heavenly Lord,
Who hath made heaven and earth of naught,
And with his blood mankind hath bought.
    Nowell, Nowell...

WE THREE KINGS

We three kings of Orient are,
Bearing gifts we travel afar,
Field and fountain, moor and mountain,
Following yonder star:
O star of wonder, star of night,
Star with royal beauty bright,
Westward leading, still proceeding,
Guide us to thy perfect light.

Born a king on Bethlehem's plain,
Gold I bring to crown him again:
King for ever, ceasing never,
Over us all to reign.
O star of wonder…

Frankincense to offer have I;
Incense owns a deity nigh:
Prayer and praising, all are raising,
Worship him, God most high.
O star of wonder…

Myrrh is mine: its bitter perfume
Breathes a life of gathering gloom;
Sorrowing, sighing, bleeding, dying,
Sealed in the stone-cold tomb.
O star of wonder…

Glorious now, behold him arise,
King and God and sacrifice.
Heaven sings, 'Alleluia!'
'Alleluia!' the earth replies.
O star of wonder…

WHILE SHEPHERDS WATCHED

While shepherds watched their flocks by night,
All seated on the ground,
The angel of the Lord came down,
And glory shone around.

'Fear not,' said he (for mighty dread
Had seized their troubled minds),
'Glad tidings of great joy I bring
To you and all mankind.

'To you in David's town this day
Is born of David's line
A Saviour, who is Christ the Lord—
And this shall be the sign:

'The heavenly babe you there shall find
To human view displayed,
All meanly wrapped in swaddling bands,
And in a manger laid.'

Thus spake the seraph, and forthwith
Appeared a shining throng
Of angels praising God, who thus
Addressed their joyful song:

'All glory be to God on high,
And to the earth be peace;
Goodwill henceforth from heaven to men
Begin and never cease.'

Reproduced with permission from *Bethlehem Carols Unpacked* published by BRF 2008 (978 1 84101 534 7)
www.barnabasinchurches.org.uk

Part Two

UNPACKING THE CAROLS

Away in a manger

STARS AND SALVATION

UNPACKING THE STORY BEHIND THE CAROL

No Christmas carol service is ever complete without this carol, not only because of the 'ahh' factor elicited by the sight of young children performing the nativity story but also because many people remember it as the first carol they themselves sang.

The first two verses of 'Away in a manger' were first published in 1885 in an American Lutheran Sunday school book. This created the misconception that the words were written by Martin Luther. The original author is, in fact, unknown. The most well-known melody, 'Cradle Song', which transformed the simple rhyme into a carol, was composed by William J. Kirkpatrick (1832–1921) in 1895, ten years after the carol was first published. Another popular melody is that of a Basque carol.

Perhaps the original author remained unaware of the fact that his or her words had become such a popular carol, which is why he or she remains, to this day, anonymous. The lyrics of the third verse (attributed to J.T. McFarland) were written ten years later than the melody, around 1906, so, 20 years from the carol's conception, it seems that the original author was still unaware of how the piece had grown. Over 100 years on, the carol remains one of the best-loved carols of all time.

UNPACKING THE BIBLICAL STORY OF THE CAROL

The words of the carol, aided and abetted by the melody, form a simple lullaby. In the tradition of most lullabies, the sentiment is sweet and syrupy—a far cry from the real setting of Jesus' birth. The first line is based on Luke 2:7. Each Christmas this verse is embellished many times over, with hosts of angels, innkeepers and their wives, donkeys, camels, shepherds, sheep and wise men all crowding on to the scene in the quest to create a part for each child in the nativity play.

The Bible verse simply says, '[Mary] gave birth to her firstborn son. She dressed him in baby clothes and laid him on a bed of hay, because there was no room for them in the inn.' The carol does not embellish the verse in the tradition of the nativity play. Instead, it homes in on the baby sleeping on his bed of hay in a rough and ready cattle trough. But there seems to be rather a lot of Vaseline on the camera lens. The reality of the event is indistinct and incomplete: the stars are twinkling in a bright sky; cattle are gently lowing; the baby doesn't cry when he wakens. It all sounds idyllically peaceful, rather like the image you might find on a Christmas card. There is no mention of the dreadful reality of a young girl, far from home, having to give birth on a cold and dirty earthen floor. Victorian propriety has sanitized the event of Jesus' birth and given it a warm and sentimental aura in the carol, suitable for delicate, well-bred children, dressed in their Sunday best.

There can be little doubt that the carol was composed with young children in mind. This theory is further supported by the animation of the stars looking down at the sleeping baby and, indeed, by the scene shift in the second verse in which Jesus himself now looks down from the sky while the child is the one sleeping—supposedly, unlike the baby Jesus, in a crib with all the trimmings.

J.T. McFarland has matched the approach of the original author in the creation of the third verse. His verse turns the carol into a simple prayer, which furthers the thought that Jesus can be near us, not only while we sleep but throughout our lives and, indeed, through all eternity. However, in the final line of this verse, we are led to suspect that a further shift of scene has taken place and the children singing the carol are now the ones looking down from the sky—their heavenly home.

This is perhaps the Peter Pan of carols—no one in it ever seems to grow up—but perhaps this is part of its appeal. It transfers a warm, sentimental glow upon us, transporting us back to our own childhood, reminding us of our own early years and, if we have reached that stage in life, those of our children or our children's children.

UNPACKING THE MEANING OF THE CAROL

Despite its sentimental feel, this carol does contain deep theological truths, especially in the third verse. As well as being the first carol that some children learn, perhaps it would be appropriate for the first two lines of verse 3 to be the very first prayer that they are taught. 'Be near me, Lord Jesus; I ask thee to stay close by me for ever, and love me, I pray' could be turned into a simple bedtime prayer, learnt by heart and called to mind in the years ahead. In theological terms, this line picks up Jesus' promise that he will be with us always, 'even until the end of the world' (Matthew 28:20). In fact, the whole carol in some ways carries out Jesus' command in the following passage:

'I have been given all authority in heaven and on earth! Go to the people of all nations and make them my disciples. Baptize them in the name of the Father, the Son, and the Holy Spirit, and teach them to do everything I have told you. I will be with you always, even until the end of the world.'
MATTHEW 28:18–20

If the words of the carol were originally written for Sunday school children, presumably they would have been within the context of biblical teaching. However, the words of this carol are well known even among those who have never attended Sunday school. Many people hear the Christmas message through this carol and are perhaps comforted by its familiarity. The original intention of the unknown author has found its place in making Jesus' promise known and fulfilling his command. How far that seed of truth has been scattered beyond the original Sunday school class!

The blessing at the end of the carol moves the child out of its immediate world to the world of those around, and draws in the story of salvation. Jesus is now not the baby laying down his sweet head but the king of heaven welcoming us into our heavenly home. Perhaps the whole story of salvation is rather a lot to draw from this simple carol but, bearing in mind the age of the original hearers and the era in which they lived, it is important to recognize that this is *implied* rather than *applied* theology. It sows the seed; the application can come later. The child learns to love Jesus, not because he or she understands the theology of salvation but because of Jesus' own love and care for the child. It is the first step in a lifetime of discovery about who Jesus is and what he has done for us and for our salvation.

In this respect, this is a 'belonging' carol, in which the steps towards 'believing' the gospel message have only just begun. Bearing this in mind, perhaps even those bright twinkling stars are not quite as sentimental as they seem, for within their imagery is the promise God first made to Abraham that he would have as many descendants as stars in the sky (Genesis 15:5). In the ancient scriptures of the Old Testament we see how from Abraham's first step of faith grew the nation of God's people. In the New Testament, we learn that those who believe the gospel message are descendants of that family and inheritors of the promise to Abraham, fulfilled in Jesus. Imbedded within the simple words of this carol is the sweep of God's great rescue plan from incarnation to ascension, from a roughly hewn cattle trough to the throne of heaven. What lullaby of love could ask for more than that the child within should be blessed with the promise of eternity?

BIBLE LINKS

The simple words of this carol pick up many biblical themes. Its childlike quality calls to mind Peter's words in his first letter: 'Be like newborn babies who are thirsty for the pure spiritual milk that will help you grow and be saved' (1 Peter 2:2). Thus we see the invitation to build on small seeds of faith and continue on the journey. Peter shows us that from the simple seeds of a newborn faith grows a spiritual house—living stones built firmly on the cornerstone of Christ:

You have already found out how good the Lord really is. Come to Jesus Christ. He is the living stone that people have rejected, but which God has chosen and highly honoured. And now you are living stones that are being used to build a spiritual house. You are also a group of holy priests, and with the help of Jesus Christ you will offer sacrifices that please God.
1 PETER 2:3–5

As the carol closes, we find a prayer of blessing, drawing us into the arms of Jesus and the promise of his kingdom. As the prayer in verse 3 implies, we are fit for heaven only through the help of Jesus Christ; with his help, we are able to become holy priests, ready to further the kingdom of God. Also, within the carol and Peter's first letter, we find an echo of Psalm 34: 'Discover for yourself that the Lord is kind. Come to him for protection, and you will be glad… If you obey the Lord, he will watch over you and answer your prayers' (vv. 8, 15), and the promise of Jesus in John's Gospel that he has prepared a place for us to be with him for ever:

'Don't be worried! Have faith in God and have faith in me. There are many rooms in my Father's house… I am going there to prepare a place for each of you. After I have done this, I will come back and take you with me. Then we will be together.'
JOHN 14:1–3

As previously mentioned, the carol also links to the following passage:

Then the Lord took Abram outside and said, "Look at the sky and see if you can count the stars. That's how many descendants you will have." Abram believed the Lord, and the Lord was pleased with him.
GENESIS 15:5–6

Finally, we cannot leave our study of the way this carol links into the Bible without bringing to mind Jesus' own attitude to children.

Some people brought their children to Jesus so that he could bless them by placing his hands on them. But his disciples told the people to stop bothering him. When Jesus saw this, he became angry and said, 'Let the children come to me! Don't try to stop them. People who are like these little children belong to the kingdom of God. I promise you that you cannot get into God's kingdom, unless you accept it the way a child does.' Then Jesus took the children in his arms and blessed them by placing his hands on them.
MARK 10:13–16

God rest you merry, gentlemen

THE MESSAGE AND THE MESSENGER

UNPACKING THE STORY BEHIND THE CAROL

The first line of the popular English carol 'God rest you merry, gentlemen' is a prime example of traditional words that we sing with no real understanding of their meaning. The sense is all down to that useful little punctuation mark, the comma. If the comma appeared after the word 'you'—'God rest you, merry gentlemen'—we might be correct in thinking that the carol is asking God to give merry gentlemen a rest. But the correct place for the comma is after the word 'merry': 'God rest you merry, gentlemen'.

'Rest you merry' is an old English phrase. The closest we come to it today is probably when we say 'rest assured', but 400 years ago it would have been a common blessing. The words call up an image of an old-fashioned Christmas. They bring to mind the scene Thomas Hardy paints at the beginning of his novel, *Under the Greenwood Tree*, with the Mellstock Quire tramping through the snow on 'a cold and starry Christmas-eve', carolling this old and well-loved message to the gentlemen of the house in return for a spot of 'good cheer' (free ale), while the ladies busy themselves in the kitchen, preparing the food for the great festival of Christmas. This might not seem politically correct to our way of thinking and, in fact, the BBC changed the line to 'God rest you merry, gentlefolk' in deference to inclusiveness when they used the carol on the TV programme *Songs of Praise*.

The carol is usually sung to the melody 'London', which is thought to have been first sung in the London streets in early Victorian times, although the words of the carol probably predate this by nearly 200 years. An earlier melody originated in Cornwall and is called 'Sandys'. The carol is still frequently sung to this version in the West Country.

UNPACKING THE BIBLICAL STORY OF THE CAROL

Once the blessing is given upon the house, the carol settles down to tell why nothing needs to dismay us at Christmas. Immediately, it reminds us that the reason we celebrate Christmas is that 'Jesus Christ our Saviour was born on Christmas Day'. The carol then tells us why this is good news, and it is the same reason given to Joseph by the angel in Matthew's Gospel: the birth of Jesus is good news because 'he will save his people from their sins' (1:21). We may all 'rest merry' (rest assured) because God's rescue plan comes into being, quite literally, through the birth of his Son.

At this point, the carol decides not to unpack the theology of salvation, choosing instead to set the scene of the birth and then tell the story of the shepherds (Luke 2:1–16). First of all, we establish that Bethlehem is in Judah, which at the time of Jesus' birth was a province of neighbouring Syria. The carol omits an explanation for why Jesus was born in Bethlehem (the census decreed by the Emperor Augustus and the long journey that Joseph, a member of the ancient bloodline of King David, had to undertake from his home town of Nazareth in order to have his details recorded at Bethlehem). Instead it moves straight to the birth itself: 'they laid him in a manger'. The last three lines of verse two seem to assume an optimism that may be just a little misplaced. It's hard to imagine that the first Christmas Day was 'this most happy morn'. The setting and circumstances surrounding Jesus' birth would surely fill any new parent with anxious concern, the noise and dirt of a draughty animal stall being far removed from what we might consider a suitable place for a tiny, vulnerable baby.

If we take time to reflect upon the physical conditions surrounding Jesus' birth, the carol may leave us wondering if Mary really did 'neither fear nor scorn' such a setting. The sentiment is in keeping with the general optimism of the carol, however, and leads nicely into the uplifting refrain, so we must take it that the writer has in mind the higher concept of God's gift of salvation through the incarnation of his Son, rather than the practical reality of Jesus' birth.

Having recounted the story of the shepherds in the next four verses, the carol concludes by turning its gaze back to the carollers. The final verse is reminiscent of the passing of the peace: 'with Christian love and fellowship each other now embrace'. Perhaps it would be good practice to conclude this carol with the passing of the peace as an outward sign of the inner truth that Christmas is a time to set aside all bitterness and to rejoice in our shared commonality under the banner of God's gift of grace.

UNPACKING THE MEANING OF THE CAROL

This carol has a subtext of salvation running through it, which is easy to miss if we concentrate solely on the familiar story of the middle verses. We shall return to the story of the shepherds but, meanwhile, let us sweep back 700 years to the message of the prophet Isaiah.

Isaiah lived in Jerusalem in the eighth century BC. Throughout his life, he was convinced of God's righteousness, warning people that God would judge their wrongdoing and comforting them with the assurance of God's love, his longing to forgive and all the good things in store for those who remained faithful to him. It is no accident that two of the lessons in a service of Nine Lessons and Carols come from the book of Isaiah. The first, Isaiah 9:2 and 6–7, heralds a message of hope, not only for those who lived through the dark days of the fall of Jerusalem, 700 years before the birth of Christ, but also for us today: 'Those who walked in the dark have seen a bright light. And it shines upon everyone who lives in the land of darkest shadows' (v. 2). These words are the underpinning for the blessing, 'God rest you merry'. They reassure us that God is in control and will act in our darkest hour. And how does he act? God acts through the gift of his Son. The words of Isaiah 9:6–7 were not originally written with the birth of Jesus in mind, but they *were* written to bear news of God's chosen one—a saviour who would dispel darkness, physically, mentally and spiritually.

The second reading from Isaiah (11:1–9) reinforces the message with further detail: he will be someone from David's family, the Spirit of the Lord will be with him to give him understanding, wisdom and insight, and he will be powerful. The passage goes on to paint an extraordinary picture of peace and harmony—leopards lying side by side with young goats, wolves resting with lambs, calves and lions eating together and little children playing near snake holes without harm. Through this powerful and extraordinary imagery, Isaiah leaves us in no doubt that the message of God's coming saviour is intrinsically linked with the message of peace.

Isaiah's message sits boldly between the story of the first sin entering the world (Genesis 3:1–19) and the coming of the Word of life at the beginning of John's Gospel (John 1:1–18). John picks up the baton of Isaiah's message and points us directly towards Jesus, whose life gives light to everyone. John's message couldn't be clearer: 'The Word became a human being and lived here with us. We saw his true glory, the glory of the only Son of the Father' (1:14). He passes the message on with a clarity that is hard to ignore.

Despite the strong biblical links found in this carol, we don't need to be theologians to pass on the good news of Jesus; we just need to have heard the story. The carol makes this crystal clear by paying no more than a fleeting visit to the theology of salvation, in favour of simply telling the Christmas story. And so we, too, are charged with telling the story; we, too, become the messengers. Just as the shepherds saw God's true glory in Bethlehem—the baby lying on a bed of hay—after hearing the song of the angels, so we, too, see God's glory through the story: the record of Jesus' life in the Gospels, the witness of his disciples and apostles, and the conviction of the Holy Spirit within us. Perhaps it is intentional that the carol picks up the shepherds' story. Like most of us, the shepherds were just ordinary people going about their daily business. They had no special status, no great wealth, no outstanding skills to equip them to pass on the message, but it was to them that God first chose to bring the message of the good news of Jesus' birth. And when they 'returned to their sheep, they were praising God and saying wonderful things about him' (Luke 2:20).

Such enthusiasm is very contagious and, although the Bible gives no further mention of the shepherds, it would be hard to believe that their life-changing encounter did not cause the message to be passed on. How good it is when we, too, are equally bursting with the good news of Jesus!

BIBLE LINKS

The following Bible links pick up the theology embedded in the carol.

Those who walked in the dark have seen a bright light. And it shines upon everyone who lives in the land of darkest shadows… A child has been born for us. We have been given a son who will be our ruler… He will always rule with honesty and justice. The Lord All-Powerful will make certain that all of this is done.

ISAIAH 9:2, 6A, 7B

Like a branch that sprouts from a stump, someone from David's family will someday be king. The Spirit of the Lord will be with him to give him understanding, wisdom, and insight… Leopards will lie down with young goats, and wolves will rest with lambs. Calves and lions will eat together and be cared for by little children. Cows and bears will share the same pasture; their young will rest side by side. Lions and oxen will both eat straw… Just as water fills the sea, the land will be filled with people who know and honour the Lord.

ISAIAH 11:1–2A, 6–7, 9B

The Word became a human being and lived here with us. We saw his true glory, the glory of the only Son of the Father. From him all the kindness and all the truth of God have come down to us.

JOHN 1:14

Good King Wenceslas

THE GIFT OF KINDNESS

UNPACKING THE STORY BEHIND THE CAROL

How on earth did this 'carol' end up in the canon of must-sing favourites at Christmas? It isn't about the Christmas story, it doesn't mention Jesus, it's based on a legend from the Czech Republic, and it's about a king who was born some eight centuries after the baby in Bethlehem. However, despite all this, it remains as popular as ever.

'Good King Wenceslas' was written by John Mason Neale and published in 1853. J.M. Neale was a prolific translator of early hymns, including the 19th-century version of the Advent antiphons ('O come, O come, Emmanuel') and 'Good Christian men, rejoice', which is based on the medieval German carol, '*In Dulci Jubilo*'. Each of these carols picks up on biblical stories. However, when he was faced with the challenge of writing something for children for the day after Christmas, Neale turned to the legend of King Wenceslas for his inspiration.

The origin of Boxing Day as an additional holiday lies in the notion of the giving of a present—a Christmas box—to those in poverty in the 'season of good will'. Indeed, an extra day off would itself have been a welcome gift for many poor people in Victorian England. The themes of riches, poverty and generosity must have become mixed in J.M. Neale's mind with the original focus for this day, which is the death of the first Christian martyr, St Stephen. This conjunction of ideas led him to the story of King Wenceslas, a tenth-century martyr in Bohemia (modern-day Czech Republic), who was well known for his acts of Christian charity.

J.M. Neale found the story in a book called *Deeds of Faith*, which was full of inspiring morality tales for children—a very popular form of literature in his day. Further inspiration may have come from John Keats' atmospheric poem 'The Eve of St Agnes', with its images of bitter cold and the poor man visiting the saint's shrine. St Agnes' fountain is mentioned in verse 2 of the carol, Agnes probably being the 13th-century local saint, Agnes of Bohemia, rather than the early Christian martyr St Agnes of Rome.

In the verses we hear a story from the life of Wenceslas (who, in fact, was not a king but a duke), when he showed kindness to a poor labourer whom he had spotted gathering wood in the bitter cold on St Stephen's day. Moved by what he saw, he set out to take a rich Christmas box of food and drink to this unfortunate individual, accompanied by his page, who, like the child for whom the carol was written, learns from the duke's example how to care for others.

For music, J.M. Neale uses a spring carol, *Tempus adest Floridum*, from the *Piae Cantiones*, a collection of medieval Latin songs published in Finland in 1582. Many later hymn writers poured scorn on Neale for spoiling a good melody with his unrhythmical and poorly scanned Wenceslas doggerel. (Incidentally, alternative Bible words for this melody were written in 1919 with the first line 'Gentle Mary laid her child'.) Nevertheless, the carol has survived such bad press and has remained known and loved to this day. It may be a piece of Victorian whimsy, but its story of generosity has continued to capture an important aspect of what Christmas means for many people. Indeed, the Bible story is perhaps here after all. There is a king who risks his life for the sake of the poor; a king who gives his followers steps in which to tread; a king who will one day be killed for doing good.

UNPACKING THE BIBLICAL STORY OF THE CAROL

It is perhaps strange that 26 December is celebrated as the feast day of St Stephen. We have no sooner marked the birth of the Saviour, with songs of glory and hope, than we are plunged straight into the story of how Stephen became the first Christian martyr—stoned to death outside Jerusalem for proclaiming Jesus Christ as Lord. Death follows hard on the heels of life and the day serves as a timely reminder that Jesus himself was born to die. It was going to be the only way he could fulfil the name of 'Jesus' that was given him (the name means 'rescuer') and the only way that Emmanuel ('God with us') could enter completely into our human story.

Stephen had great faith and was filled with the Holy Spirit (Acts 6:5). He was the person used by God to tell the spiritual leaders of his day that God's Spirit does not live in a building made by humans (7:48). When faced with his persecutors, he gave a full and measured picture of the true history of God's people and boldly told the members of the Jewish council that they needed to put their faith in Jesus as Messiah. Stephen spoke with the great wisdom that God had given him (6:10) and was used by God to show those who took stones to kill him that God's power is made perfect in weakness. Here was a man who, in every sense, was fully alive in Christ and yet emptied himself completely so that others— including Saul, who later became the apostle Paul and a leader of the early Church—would see what God was truly like.

Stephen was convinced that he had heard God's voice in the life, death and resurrection of Jesus. He was prepared to follow that voice wherever it led and whatever the cost. Faith in Jesus for him meant choosing to live with one foot on earth and one in heaven, so death was not an end but merely the next step on his journey to be with God. His unshakeable belief in the divinity of Jesus shone out, even before his trial started (6:15). His accusers noted how the light of heaven was already in his face and, by the end of the proceedings, Stephen could confidently exclaim that he saw heaven's door open and the Son of Man standing at the right side of God (7:56).

Wenceslas' death is not so well documented, but he too was a martyr for the Christian faith. He was killed by his own brother, who later repented and became a Christian (rather in the way that Saul became a follower of Jesus after his Damascus road experience). Wenceslas, or Vaclav as he is known in his own native language, is today the patron saint of the Czech Republic. There is a statue to him in Wenceslas Square in the centre of Prague and it was in this square, in more recent times, that the Czech people stood up to the communist government that had kept their country behind the 'iron curtain' after World War II.

Kindness and caring for others, as the mark of those who follow the true king, is also a theme that is repeated throughout the teaching of the Gospels and perhaps most powerfully in the parable of the final judgment (Matthew 25:31–46). In this chilling story, Jesus describes how the king will deal with his subjects depending on how they have used the gift of life that has been theirs. They fall into two groups. The sheep earn the king's approval because they have cared for those in need, whereas the goats have failed to show such kindness.

The remarkable truth contained in this parable is that, in caring for other people, the king's subjects have actually been caring for the king himself. He says, 'Whenever you did it for any of my people, no matter how unimportant they seemed, you did it for me' (v. 40). Christians are urged to see Christ in everyone and most especially in the lives of those who are in any kind of need.

The truth of this story is well expressed in a Christmas poem by David Adam, written in the Celtic style.

Christmas poor

You are the caller
You are the poor
You are the stranger at my door

You are the wanderer
You are the unfed
You are the homeless with no bed

You are the man
Driven insane
You are the child
Crying in pain

You are the other, who comes to me
If I open to another, you are born in me

DAVID ADAM, *THE EDGE OF GLORY:*
PRAYERS IN THE CELTIC TRADITION (TRIANGLE, 1985)

'Good King Wenceslas' focuses on this biblical message for Christmas: to follow the baby king will be costly and will mean stepping out from the safety of whatever 'palace' we occupy, to reach out and show kindness to those who are in need of God's love. This is both the genuine mark and the sure test of true Christian discipleship.

UNPACKING THE MEANING OF THE CAROL

Another king at Christmas? There's already King Herod in the Bible story, plus the 'three kings' (although we don't know that there were three, nor that they were kings), and Jesus himself is the baby king; so to introduce King Wenceslas into the mix is possibly one king too many! However, this may be more justified than it seems at first.

For Christians, the birth of Jesus is a unique and world-changing moment in the whole history of creation. Human civilization is often characterized by a procession of kings and queens—dynasties and royal families who lend their names to epochs and empires. History is written by them and for them and we are in danger of seeing our human story only through their regal eyes. Some, like King Herod, are tyrants; some, like the wise men, have been more kindly leaders and seekers after truth; and some, like Wenceslas, have become examples for us to follow. Wenceslas' kingship was like this, however, because he modelled his life on the true king. Jesus is the servant king who sets us an example to follow (see 1 Peter 2:18–21), just as Wenceslas' boot-deep footprints marked a safe way through the treacherous snow for his loyal page.

All Christians are called to 'mark well the master's steps', as the carol reminds us. St Stephen (whose name, incidentally, means 'crown': it seems we have even more kings to consider!) chose to follow in Jesus' footsteps and he, like the page in the tale, began by waiting on tables as a deacon.

The Christmas story and the Boxing Day legend enshrined in this carol remind us what sort of king God is. He is a king who is high above the heavens, but also 'lifts the poor and needy from dust and ashes' (Psalm 113:7); a king who helps everyone who is weak (just as Paul urges his listeners to do in Acts 20:35); a king whose love and faithfulness will last for ever (Psalm 100:5). Indeed, another king, King Solomon, made that clear when he wrote, 'Kings who are fair to the poor will rule for ever' (Proverbs 29:14), and the last lines of this carol are based on yet another king's discovery, this time King David, who proclaimed, 'You, Lord God, bless everyone who cares for the poor, and you rescue those people in times of trouble' (Psalm 41:1).

At a time of year when so many of us are seduced into spending excessive amounts of money on our families and ourselves rather than those in need, this carol reminds us that King David's greater Son calls us to be subjects of a new sort of king, who came to turn our ideas of wealth and poverty upside down. Paul writes of this king, 'You know that our Lord Jesus Christ was kind enough to give up all his riches and become poor, so that you could become rich (2 Corinthians 8:9).

BIBLE LINKS

Either of the following two passages would be appropriate Bible readings to accompany this carol.

- Acts 6:1—7:60 (the story of Stephen)
- Matthew 25:31–46 (the parable of the sheep and goats)

The story of Stephen's ministry, arrest, trial and death is, however, too long to use in a service and so it would probably be best to focus either on the description of his life and service as a deacon in Acts 6:1–5 or on his bold and gifted preaching, which draws the unwelcome attention of the authorities in Acts 6:8–15.

The parable of the sheep and the goats is also headed 'the final judgment' in some Bibles. This, too, is a fairly long and challenging passage. However, the story of Good King Wenceslas particularly picks up the king's words to the sheep, so an appropriate shorter version of this reading could be Matthew 25:31–40.

Hark! the herald-angels sing

LIGHT AND LIFE

UNPACKING THE STORY BEHIND THE CAROL

Would you call it collaborative creativity or one of the longest editing processes ever? 'Hark! the herald-angels sing', or ''Ark-the-errald' as it is known to carol singers, is a joint venture, stretching over 150 years, as the words and music have been rewritten over and over again. Perhaps we have done the carol a disservice by setting it in stone: could someone in your congregation improve on it to stretch the process even further across time?

In 1739, the great and prolific hymn writer Charles Wesley, brother of John, wrote the words with their rich scriptural resonance. The original words were slightly different from those we now sing. It originally began 'Hark! How all the welkin rings / Glory to the king of kings…' ('welkin' meaning 'sky'). The legend is that Wesley wrote them on a starry Christmas eve while travelling to a midnight service on horseback.

In 1753, George Whitefield changed the words of the first two lines to what we now sing and, in 1760, Martin Madan rewrote other parts of the carol and added several new verses. In 1855, William Hayman Cummings adapted a chorus from Mendelssohn's secular oratorio *Festgesang* (1844) to provide a suitably joyous accompaniment. In 1889, the original ten verses were shortened to four, which almost exactly correspond to the original version, but most carol books today reduce the number of verses to just three. It's a joint effort, if ever there was one, but surely both Charles Wesley and Mendelssohn would have been delighted that so many people from all traditions know and love the carol in its present form.

UNPACKING THE BIBLICAL STORY OF THE CAROL

The carol focuses less on the story surrounding Jesus' birth and more on the wonder and meaning of the incarnation. It takes an imaginative interpretation of the triumphant words of the angels to the shepherds as its starting point and returns to them with ever-increasing wonder at the end of each verse. The relevant passage of the Bible is as follows:

That night in the fields near Bethlehem some shepherds were guarding their sheep. All at once an angel came down to them from the Lord, and the brightness of the Lord's glory flashed around them. The shepherds were frightened. But the angel said, 'Don't be afraid! I have good news for you, which will make everyone happy. This very day in King David's home town a Saviour was born for you. He is Christ the Lord. You will know who he is, because you will find him dressed in baby clothes and lying on a bed of hay.' Suddenly many other angels came down from heaven and joined in praising God. They said: 'Praise God in heaven! Peace on earth to everyone who pleases God!'
LUKE 2:8–14

It's a picture of a dark hillside made busy by the pastoral industry of raising sheep—perhaps for the Passover festival. The shepherds were outsiders whose lives were reputed to be so shifty and unreliable that they were not permitted to give testimony in a court of law. This dark scene is then transformed by the arrival of an angel and by the glory that surrounds the shepherds themselves. It is reminiscent of the Lord coming down in clouds of glory on Mount Sinai to give Moses the Ten Commandments (Exodus 19:18).

How often have we thought of the glory emanating from the angel? Luke describes the glory as something that flashes around the *shepherds*. Something radical has shifted since the time described in Exodus 19: now the glory of the Lord can come down on a mountain without killing either flocks or people who weren't 'acceptable'.

While the angels don't actually sing, 'Glory to the newborn king' as the carol interprets it, they do give glory to God in highest heaven first, knowing that their vision of 'peace on earth' cannot come until glory is given to God on earth as in heaven. Perhaps the scene on the hillside can be considered as a tiny depiction of God's kingdom coming to earth, as those at the bottom of the pile in human terms are bathed in God's glory and given responsibilities over and above anything that human society is prepared to give them.

UNPACKING THE MEANING OF THE CAROL

What is the carol about, as we know it today in the three verses in our carol sheets? It doesn't tell a story, as so many of our popular carols do; rather, it is a song of praise, catching us up in the wonder of Jesus' birth. This praise begins with the angels' praise. From the very first line, it is as if the herald angels are actually singing here and now, compelling us to listen: 'Hark!' They invite everyone all over the world to join with them to create a great hymn of praise to God from both earth and heaven.

Why is this baby's birth so important? Verse 2 gets excited about the mystery of the majestic and glorious Son of God choosing to hide his divinity in a human body and become a human baby so that he can truly be Emmanuel: 'God with us'. Are we singing to Christ directly or inviting each other to 'behold him come' and 'see' him? It's not clear, especially in the thrill of singing the lines, but in a way that's all the more exciting. It's as if we are so overjoyed by the wonder of his birth that we are like the shepherds, praising God and wondering about it together, all at the same time.

Finally, in the third verse, we shout unambiguous praise to this Prince of Peace, the Sun of Righteousness, greeting him as he arrives on earth as a king or emperor: 'Hail!' Again, the sense is very immediate. Christmas is happening here and now, not just two thousand years ago. The praise increases as we sing of the real message of Christ's coming—our salvation, which his death on the cross will bring.

The updating of 'Born that man no more may die' to 'Born that we no more may die' dilutes the statuesque grandeur of the last three lines and sits oddly with the more traditional 'sons of earth', but that is the compromise made to bring the words slightly more in line with present-day linguistic sensibilities. And we finish with a rousing repeat of the chorus: a call to celebrate peace between nations and between God and humanity. It becomes a joyful declaration that the most high God has come to earth as a human being, and a rousing cheer that he came to bring light, healing, peace, mercy and new life to those of us on earth. As we sing it, it is an uplifting affirmation of 'light and life' that Jesus came to bring. You can almost hear the trumpets!

BIBLE LINKS

There are many references to light in the Bible. The light of life bursts forth at the beginning of creation and shines out in God's gift of Jesus and his promise of new creation. The light of Jesus is the light of life, entrusted to us as inheritors of God's kingdom and conduits of his light in the world. A selection of the following Bible verses could be used as a creative way to set the scene for the service.

God said, 'I command light to shine!' And light started shining. God looked at the light and saw that it was good.
GENESIS 1:3–4A

You, Lord, are the light that keeps me safe.
PSALM 27:1A

Your love is a treasure, and everyone finds shelter in the shadow of your wings. You give your guests a feast in your house, and you serve a tasty drink that flows like a river. The life-giving fountain belongs to you, and your light gives light to each of us.
PSALM 36:7–9

I praise you, Lord God, with all my heart. You are glorious and majestic, dressed in royal robes and surrounded by light.
PSALM 104:1–2A

Your word is a lamp that gives light wherever I walk.
PSALM 119:105

Those who walked in the dark have seen a bright light. And it shines upon everyone who lives in the land of darkest shadows.
ISAIAH 9:2

Give your food to the hungry and care for the homeless. Then your light will shine in the dark.
ISAIAH 58:10

Jerusalem, stand up! Shine! Your new day is dawning. The glory of the Lord shines brightly on you. The earth and its people are covered with darkness, but the glory of the Lord is shining upon you.
ISAIAH 60:1–2

You won't need the light of the sun or the moon. I, the Lord your God, will be your eternal light and bring you honour. Your sun will never set or your moon go down. I, the Lord, will be your everlasting light, and your days of sorrow will come to an end.
ISAIAH 60:19–20

The light keeps shining in the dark, and darkness has never put it out.
JOHN 1:5

Once again Jesus spoke to the people. This time he said, 'I am the light for the world! Follow me, and you won't be walking in the dark. You will have the light that gives life.'
JOHN 8:12

Try to shine as lights among the people of this world, as you hold firmly to the message that gives life.
PHILIPPIANS 2:15B–16A

But you are God's chosen and special people. You are a group of royal priests and a holy nation. God has brought you out of darkness into his marvellous light.
1 PETER 2:9

O come, all ye faithful

THE INVITATION

This carol is not all that it seems! The melody is known as *Adeste Fideles*, which is Latin for the first line of the song. From this we might conclude that it has its roots in the Middle Ages, when Latin was the language of the Church. Indeed, in some carol collections you will find the Latin text.

But don't let all this Latin fool you! The carol is believed to have been written in France in about 1743 by John F. Wade, who was a Roman Catholic layman and a classical scholar with a great interest in plainsong and music. The English words were translated from John Wade's Latin, almost one hundred years later, by the Anglican clergyman Frederick Oakley. The original Latin has successfully misled some people, however, and today you may find this carol attributed to monks from the Middle Ages, even St Bonaventura himself, who was a successor to St Francis and bishop of Albano.

The original version had just four verses, and this is the one most frequently used today. There were, however, a great number of variant verses—38 versions in total. A longer version that appears in several hymn books and is used popularly on Christmas Day adds three verses in the centre of the original four, which were translated in 1884 by W.T. Brooke. They refer to the visit of the shepherds ('See how the shepherds, summoned to his cradle'), the Epiphany ('Lo, star-led chieftains, Magi, Christ adoring') and our redemption,

('Child for us sinners… Who would not love thee, loving us so dearly?').

In another twist of confusion to this carol's origins, it is also known as the Portuguese Hymn. This nickname arises from the fact that the Duke of Leeds, who was a prominent Roman Catholic at the end of the 18th century, organized a private hearing of this 'new' carol to be performed in the Portuguese Embassy in London. He mistakenly thought that it had come from Portugal.

The melody is less easy to track down, but was probably also written by J.F. Wade. What a mixed and deceptive parentage this carol has had! It is filled with movement and is therefore often used as a processional at midnight mass on Christmas eve.

UNPACKING THE BIBLICAL STORY OF THE CAROL

The longer version of the carol tells the whole Christmas story. In the verse that begins, 'See how the shepherds, summoned to his cradle', we are urged to join the shepherds as they hurry to Bethlehem: 'We too will thither bend our joyful footsteps.' This reminds us of the different journeys involved in the Christmas story: our imaginative journey ('Come all ye faithful… come ye to Bethlehem'), God's journey from heaven to earth ('God from God… lo, he abhors not the Virgin's womb'), the angels' journey from heaven to the shepherds' fields and, in the Epiphany verse, the wise men's journey ('We to the Christ child bring our hearts' oblation').

The carol is an invitation to step into the nativity story, to make our own journey of the imagination to be there in the Bethlehem stable, and to join our worship with that of the others who have already travelled to this place. The repeated chorus gives added urgency to the invitation to be there.

God has travelled, too, according to verse 2, from heaven to the hay. Jesus is God, arrived on earth as a child—perfect God and perfect human. The angels sing to God in the highest (verse 3) and to the baby, who is described as the king of the angels (verse 1). In fact, all of heaven is involved in the celebration and so we are invited to join them.

The carol invites us to meet and greet God's arrival for ourselves, to respond to the wonder of this unique event with adoration. The carol culminates in a great 'yes' and gives us words to respond for ourselves to the invitation to see, sing and meet the mystery of the incarnation.

Verse 2 is notoriously difficult to sing without getting the scansion wrong and it is also full of theological soundbite ('God from God', 'Light from Light') as well as some archaic language ('abhors', 'begotten'). As such, this verse is a musical version of the Nicene Creed, with its carefully worded phrases that assert Jesus' identity as both God and man—a rebuff to the heresy that denies his place as the second person of the Trinity.

The repeated chorus line is successful in helping the singers and listeners to feel drawn into the wonder and glory of the incarnation. Its rising volume, often accompanied by descants, is calculated to stir the spirit of the most hard-hearted Scrooge! Its crescendo of praise gives us a reason to be there and respond to this urgent invitation.

The climax is the special Christmas Day verse, which we at last sing on the day itself to make public the fact that we have arrived at the end of our journey, along with the shepherds and wise men. The journey we have undertaken in response to the invitation is over.

UNPACKING THE MEANING OF THE CAROL

This carol is one that we are definitely singing to each other at Christmas, in order to encourage everyone to celebrate the miracle of the incarnation. It is unashamedly upbeat and allows for no doubting or hesitation in our commitment to praise. The Christian truth of Christmas is something worth shouting triumphantly about, in chords that must drown out any other voices that threaten to rob this festival of its true meaning. As such, it is a robust counterblast to the ringing of high street tills, the revelry of office parties and the blare of television schedules, which seem so completely to have taken over Christmas in our day and age.

The carol pulls no punches, either, about why Christmas is so special. It goes straight to the heart of the mystery of the incarnation. It is sung theology, borrowing words from the credal statements of our faith and turning them into song. Christmas isn't just a spot of light relief in the darkness of winter (in the northern hemisphere, at least); it is about an event that reverberates in heaven and across time. The carol takes eternity as its setting and reminds us that angels, archangels and all the company of heaven are involved ('sing, choirs of angels… sing, all ye citizens of heaven above')—picking up words that are drawn from the liturgy of Holy Communion.

'O come, all ye faithful' strikes a high note of pure celebration; no wonder it is often used as the opening song to set the scene for the whole carol service, and is frequently sung at the end of a midnight service to welcome Christmas Day. The chorus of 'O come, let us adore him' is not just for the one day of Christmas or the one event of the baby in the manger, but it is for all people, in all places and at all times. Here is a chorus that Christians can sing again and again on any day of the year and throughout their whole lives. Quite simply, it's a carol that is not just for Christmas.

BIBLE LINKS

The story of the carol is based on the account of the birth of Jesus in Luke 2:1–20. The words of verse 2 in particular owe much to John 1:1–14, especially verse 14, which tells us that the Word became a human being. The God who is light becomes a child.

The Word became a human being and lived here with us. We saw his true glory, the glory of the only Son of the Father. From him all the kindness and all the truth of God have come down to us.

JOHN 1:14

O little town of Bethlehem

THE HEART OF THE STORY

UNPACKING THE STORY BEHIND THE CAROL

'O little town of Bethlehem' is probably America's favourite carol. It was written shortly after the Civil War in 1868 by the Rector of Holy Trinity Church, Philadelphia, Phillips Brooks. He was inspired by his visit to the Holy Land three years earlier, when, on Christmas eve, he had stood on the traditional site of the shepherds' fields and looked out over Bethlehem. Afterwards he had joined in a five-hour church service and had been captivated by the powerful singing in that special place. In his journal he wrote:

I remember standing in the old church, close to the spot where Jesus was born, when the whole church was ringing hour after hour with splendid hymns of praise to God, how again and again it seemed as if I could hear voices I knew well, telling each other of the wonderful night of the Saviour's birth.

Back home, it was Brooks' organist, Lewis Redner, a successful local estate agent and also a leader of the Sunday school, who composed the tune, 'St Louis', which is now widely used in the States. He wrote this music on Christmas eve and then rehearsed it to be performed by the Sunday school the following day. The carol truly is a Christmas eve inspiration.

In England, the folk melody 'Forest Green', arranged by Ralph

Vaughan Williams, is most often used for this carol. A delicate melody by Walford Davies is also found in several carol books and is sometimes used at the service of Nine Lessons and Carols in King's College, Cambridge.

UNPACKING THE BIBLICAL STORY OF THE CAROL

The words of the carol capture the Christian truth that Bethlehem became a meeting place for all our longings ('the hopes and fears of all the years are met in thee tonight') and God's gracious response in giving us Jesus ('the wondrous gift'). Earth remains silent and unaware of the enormity of what is happening. It is only the stars and the angels that can't help but burst into song ('O morning stars, together proclaim the holy birth'; 'we hear the Christmas angels'). In summary, the carol is quite simply saying, 'Christmas isn't Christmas until it happens in your heart.'

The carol breathes silence and stillness. It asks to be sung in hushed, reverential tones—all of it, not just verse 3. Most people are sleeping, we are told, and the streets are silent. Even the stars are silent. The arrival of God on earth causes them to break into song. Jesus is portrayed in affectionate and gentle language. He is the holy child, the dear Christ, the wondrous gift and our Lord Emmanuel.

UNPACKING THE MEANING OF THE CAROL

'O little town of Bethlehem' tries to capture the mystery and meaning of what was happening on that first Christmas. It begins in a specific geographical location but ends in a spiritual place. Bethlehem's streets beneath the stars become our hearts beneath our hopes and fears. Something eternal can happen for everyone, the carol is saying, made possible by this birth. Jesus is born of Mary, and his birth becomes a metaphor for the spiritual rebirth that we all need in order to discover the intimacy of God in our lives.

It is a carol that takes the singer from the external facts to the Christian truth behind this historical event. It gives us words to make a personal commitment to God as we receive Christ for ourselves through faith. It talks of his 'coming', his 'being born in us' and his 'abiding with us'. All this picks up on language used later in Jesus' ministry, reflecting how we need to enter and live in the kingdom that he introduces.

BIBLE LINKS

This carol is a wonderful opportunity to focus on the prophecy about Bethlehem as the promised place where the Messiah would be born.

Bethlehem Ephrath, you are one of the smallest towns in the nation of Judah. But the Lord will choose one of your people to rule the nation—someone whose family goes back to ancient times.
MICAH 5:2

Herod brought together the chief priests and the teachers of the Law of Moses and asked them, 'Where will the Messiah be born?' They told him, 'He will be born in Bethlehem, just as the prophets wrote, "Bethlehem in the land of Judah, you are very important among the towns of Judea. From your town will come a leader, who will be like a shepherd for my people Israel."'
MATTHEW 2:4–6

Once in royal David's city

RICHES AND POVERTY

UNPACKING THE STORY BEHIND THE CAROL

Mrs Cecil Frances Alexander, the wife of the Bishop of Derry (later Archbishop of Armagh), who had been writing religious verse since the age of nine, published this carol in 1848 in her collection *Hymns for Little Children*. The book was so successful that it was reprinted 69 times before the end of the 19th century, Mrs Alexander donating the proceeds to her own charity for the deaf. Three of her hymns based on the Creed: 'All things bright and beautiful' (creation), 'Once in royal David's city' (incarnation) and 'There is a green hill far away' (crucifixion), are still widely known and loved.

In 1849, H.J. Gauntlett, one of the leading Victorian organists and composers of hymn tunes, set 'Once in royal David's city' to the melody 'Irby'.

UNPACKING THE BIBLICAL STORY OF THE CAROL

The carol concentrates on the obscure birth of Jesus into a low-income household. Luke writes, 'She gave birth to her firstborn son. She dressed him in baby clothes and laid him on a bed of hay, because there was no room for them in the inn' (2:7). Whether Mary and Joseph ended up in an inn's stable in Bethlehem or in a relative's house where the animals used the same building as the family, the picture is still one of poverty, exclusion, discomfort and danger. In a world where the majority of the population still live below the poverty line, this scene is one of God identifying himself with humanity at its most deprived and vulnerable.

It is also a picture of God trusting human beings with a crucial job. The roles are reversed as human beings are asked to do God's work for him. Just as God gave birth to the world, Mary gives birth to Jesus. Then we have the puzzling, touching detail of her dressing the baby. Why does Luke include this detail? Isn't it an obvious thing to do as a baby arrives in the world? Seen from the wider biblical perspective, however, it makes sense. In this topsy-turvy Christmas story, Mary dresses Jesus just as God dressed Adam and Eve as they left the safety of Eden and went out into the wilderness. Then she makes a desperate situation as comfortable for the baby as she can by laying him on a bed of hay. She does the best she can in an impossible situation, according to her ability and wisdom, and that is good enough for God. If he wanted perfection, he would surely do it all himself. God gives the most important job in history to a teenage girl who had the faith and trust to say 'Yes' to him.

UNPACKING THE MEANING OF THE CAROL

Alone among the carols we have come to associate with Christmas, 'Once in royal David's city' uses the birth of Jesus as a starting point to meditate upon the life of Jesus as a young child and his imagined relationship beyond babyhood with Mary. The writer imagines Jesus' obedience, meekness and respect for his mother, dwells briefly on his ability to empathize with Victorian children in good times and bad, and reassures children of life after death. A thread running through the song is the lowliness of the baby's birth, upbringing and choice of company compared with his position as 'God and Lord of all': the word 'lowly' is used no less than four times.

This carol is a superb example of simplicity of language and communication with a young audience. Most of the words have just one syllable; hardly any have more than two. The narrative is clear and enthralling. A couple of lines, however, give a fascinating Victorian view of childhood. While telling the story of the birth of Jesus in simple and vivid language, Mrs Alexander breaks off the narrative to moralize about the expected behaviour of Christian children ('Christian children all must be mild, obedient, good as he'). For her, high spirits and energetic behaviour have no part in the life of a Christian child. Jesus lies in Mary's 'gentle arms', loving and watching her, honouring and obeying her. This refers directly to Luke's narrative of Jesus being lost in the temple—'Jesus went back to Nazareth with his parents and obeyed them' (2:51)—as well as the fifth of the Ten Commandments, 'Respect your father and mother' (Deuteronomy 5:16).

It is interesting, too, that the carol starts with birth and finishes with death, with no mention of the adult Christ, the cross or resurrection in between. 'Redeeming love' is the nearest reference to the events of Good Friday. Death was often tragically close to birth in the Victorian period and it was as well to be prepared for it from an early age. The concept of heaven is simplified for this childish audience to a geographical place 'on high', where children will be wearing white and crowned like stars, surely a reference to Revelation 7:9: 'I saw a large crowd with more people than could be counted. They were from every race, tribe, nation, and language, and they stood before the throne and before the Lamb. They wore white robes and held palm branches in their hands.'

Is this a deliberate idealization of childhood to give hope and vision to the many children of Victorian times who struggled with appalling home conditions, were sent out to work in the mills and chimneys and sculleries, and were often viewed as expendable? Or is it an affirmation that children should be valued because the Son of God was also a child?

Mrs Alexander was a woman of her age and social background.

Although the words and sentiments may seem rather precious to our ears, she was a pioneer in the Sunday school movement, writing a large number of hymns especially for children, as an attempt to teach the Christian faith in words that they could understand and remember. Millions of people, both then and today, must have received their first image of the nativity and their confidence of enjoying the presence of God in heaven from this poem.

'Once in royal David's city' will be sung this Christmas in King's College, Cambridge and beyond, and will bring many a tear to many an eye. By some strange alchemy, it evokes snow falling on cottage rooftops and people in muffs skipping through frosted landscapes to their village church on Christmas morning.

BIBLE LINKS

This carol, like so many, has echoes of well-trodden themes throughout both Old and New Testaments. The emphasis on Jesus' earthly poverty, his concern for the poor and his identification with them rather than with the rich comes through loud and clear. In the Bible, this theme occurs in many passages, including Mary's song in Luke 1:46–55; Isaiah 11:4, where we read, 'The poor and the needy will be treated with fairness and with justice'; and Isaiah 53:3b: 'We despised him and said, "He is a nobody!"' In his lifetime, Jesus was sometimes seen as a very ordinary person. Mark reports, 'Many of the people who heard him were amazed and asked, "How can he do all this? Where did he get such wisdom and the power to perform these miracles? Isn't he the carpenter, the son of Mary?"' (6:2–3). The idea of a prince disguised in rags, living and identifying with the poor, has strong echoes in the Christmas story. It reminds us, in our mainly affluent Western society, that this story belongs to the oppressed and exploited from all over the globe.

The theme of Jesus growing up as an ordinary child, going through the heartaches and joys of childhood, forms the core of the carol, and is echoed in Luke 2:40: 'The child Jesus grew. He became strong and wise, and God blessed him.' If we can stretch childhood to the age of twelve and above (which, admittedly, is beyond what might have been the expectation of Jesus' community), Luke adds, 'Jesus went back to Nazareth with his parents and obeyed them… Jesus became wise, and he grew strong. God was pleased with him and so were the people' (Luke 2:51–52).

Perhaps children find it helpful to know that Jesus also experienced what it is like to be a child. Perhaps it helps us to understand the value God places on childhood and children when we see that he was prepared to go through that process himself, rather than spring into the world as a fully formed adult. For all societies where children are considered worthless or expendable, this is a reminder that childhood has dignity and value simply because God chose to enter that state himself. His understanding of the human condition comes across in Hebrews 4:15: 'Jesus understands every weakness of ours, because he was tempted in every way that we are. But he did not sin!'

Mrs Alexander also gives us glimpses of the afterlife, where the poverty of earth has been transformed to the glory of heaven. It is a verse designed to give reassurance about heaven, about our reception there by Jesus himself and a sense of the clean, bright majesty of our eternal home. Jesus himself reassured his nervous followers, 'Don't be worried! Have faith in God and have faith in me. There are many rooms in my Father's house… I am going there to prepare a place for each of you. After I have done this, I will come back and take you with me. Then we will be together' (John 14:1–3).

The once-poor Jesus will be at God's right hand, just as the apostle Stephen claimed to have seen him just before he was stoned to death by members of the Jewish council. 'Then Stephen said, "I see heaven open and the Son of Man standing at the right side of God!"' (Acts 7:56). The white clothes and crowns are reminiscent of the elders and martyrs in the book of Revelation: 'on each of these thrones there was an elder dressed in white clothes and wearing a gold crown' (4:4) and '[the martyrs] stood before the throne and before the Lamb. They wore white robes and held palm branches in their hands' (7:9).

The carol gives hope to those who are marginalized by society—a reminder that God himself chose to become as 'worthless' as a child, to live a life of poverty and deprivation, and that eventually he gained the prize of eternal glory, just as his faithful followers will.

Silent night

REDEEMING GRACE

UNPACKING THE STORY BEHIND THE CAROL

The picturesque legend that has grown up alongside 'Silent night' tells of an Austrian parish priest, Joseph Mohr, who found to his horror that, on Christmas eve itself, the bellows of his church organ had been nibbled by mice. No organ! No music! A major festival! What a disaster! Acting swiftly, the priest remembered a poem he had written some time before—a simple poem, perhaps too simple for such a great festival. He rushed to his friend Franz Gruber and explained the crisis. Gruber pulled out a guitar and, within hours, had composed the simple haunting melody in time for the Christmas mass. The day was saved, and arguably the most famous of all carols was born. The legend continues that the carol was lost and all but forgotten until its manuscript was discovered in 1825 by a workman repairing the church organ.

What we do know is that the original German words for the carol were written in 1816 by Joseph Mohr and the music composed around 1818 by Franz Gruber. The parish of Nicola Kirche of Oberndorf in Austria first sang the carol around this period. The melody is in the style of many German folk melodies, is based on just three chords and is suitable for strumming on a guitar.

Since then, 'Silent night' has spread around the world. Perhaps its most legendary moment after its conception is the supposed singing of 'Silent night' and, in German, *'Stille Nacht'* in the trenches on Christmas Eve 1914 by German and British troops. However, although eyewitness accounts certainly recall carols being sung, and even mention some by name (such as 'The first Nowell' and 'Adeste fideles'), there does not seem to be a contemporary mention of 'Silent night'. Perhaps it was really sung in the trenches or perhaps, even more interestingly, it is a measure of the carol's mythical properties that we feel it *should* have been sung at such a time of conflict, showing powerfully the message of peace and reconciliation for which the world was longing.

It is often seen as the 'archetypal' Christmas carol, right up to its appearance in the 21st-century film *Love Actually*, where the lovestruck hero stands at his best friend's door playing 'Silent night' on his CD player to feign the presence of carol singers, declaring through placards his hopeless love for his best friend's wife.

UNPACKING THE BIBLICAL STORY OF THE CAROL

Perhaps this carol is most remarkable for what it excludes of the 'full' Christmas story. It is pared down to a vision of the mother and child in the stable at night and the angels coming to the shepherds on the hillside, which can all be found in a few verses from Luke 2. There is no mention of Joseph, the journey to Bethlehem or what the shepherds did after they had heard the angels, let alone the visit of the magi, as we find in some other carols.

UNPACKING THE MEANING OF THE CAROL

In the translation in the *Bethlehem Carol Sheet*, a picture is painted of a moment of stillness and silence at the manger of the newborn baby. It is as if nothing else exists: even Joseph isn't included. There are no animals, nothing in the first verse except Mary and Jesus in a pool of light, which seems to be a circle of peace and protection, letting them sleep within it. The second verse links the stable to the scene outside Bethlehem on the hillside, but although it describes a loud, brilliant event, with shepherds quailing and all the dynamics of glory streaming from heaven, the lilting music distances us from any emotional involvement. All is still gentle and we return almost gratefully from this intrusion of the outside world to the third verse and the even tighter focus of the baby's face itself, the source of the light in verse 1. With the build-up of light images, the song ends in a description of the light that Christ will bring to the dark world, with all the gentleness of the dawn changing the night to day.

The power of this most famous of carols lies in the haunting simplicity of its melody and the evocation of a moment of stillness, which is perhaps an echo of our longing for the deep peace of true worship.

BIBLE LINKS

The carol picks up the themes of the virgin mother, the image of dark turning to dawn, peace, trust, stillness, grace and redemption. The scene of the carol comes from Luke 2. For further study, the book of Ruth explores the theme of the 'kinsman redeemer'.

A virgin is pregnant; she will have a son and will name him Immanuel.
ISAIAH 7:14

Those who walked in the dark have seen a bright light.
ISAIAH 9:2A

The lifestyle of good people is like sunlight at dawn that keeps getting brighter until broad daylight.
PROVERBS 4:18

Once again Jesus spoke to the people. This time he said, 'I am the light for the world! Follow me, and you won't be walking in the dark. You will have the light that gives life.'
JOHN 8:12

I pray that your love will keep on growing and that you will fully know and understand how to make the right choices. Then you will still be pure and innocent when Christ returns. And until that day, Jesus Christ will keep you busy doing good deeds that bring glory and praise to God.
PHILIPPIANS 1:9–11

You are God's children. He sent Christ Jesus to save us and to make us wise, acceptable, and holy.
1 CORINTHIANS 1:30

Then Christ went once for all into the most holy place and freed us from sin for ever. He did this by offering his own blood instead of the blood of goats and bulls.
HEBREWS 9:12

[Jesus said] 'If you are tired from carrying heavy burdens, come to me and I will give you rest. Take the yoke I give you. Put it on your shoulders and learn from me. I am gentle and humble, and you will find rest. This yoke is easy to bear, and this burden is light.'
MATTHEW 11:28–30

I pray that the Lord, who gives peace, will always bless you with peace. May the Lord be with all of you.
2 THESSALONIANS 3:16

Jesus got up and ordered the wind and waves to stop. They obeyed, and everything was calm. Then Jesus asked the disciples, 'Don't you have any faith?'
LUKE 8:24B–25A

The Lord is your protector, and he won't go to sleep or let you stumble. The protector of Israel doesn't doze or ever get drowsy.
PSALM 121:3–4

The first Nowell

OUTSIDE IN

UNPACKING THE STORY BEHIND THE CAROL

Everybody has an opinion on the meaning of the most repeated word in this carol. As mentioned in the Introduction, *Noël* is French for 'Christmas', which suggests that the word 'Nowell' had Norman origins. Latin scholars trace its roots further back to *dies natalis*, which means 'birthday': over the years, *natalis* may have been corrupted to become 'noël'. Some language experts, however, claim that 'nowells' is a medieval English word meaning 'news'. There are also suggestions that the word may have ancient origins in its association with the Franco-Germanic words for 'new' (*neu*) and 'light' (*helle*). All this speculation explains the wide variety of spellings for this important word. Interestingly, however, a Cornish version solves the disputes rather neatly by rendering 'noel' as 'Oh well'!

It is perhaps no surprise, therefore, that the original author of this carol remains a mystery, but he or she may well have lived as far back as the 13th century. The carol first appeared in a collection printed by William Sandy in 1833. There are a whole host of versions, along with many alternative or additional verses so that the singers can tell more and more of the Christmas story. Another traditional carol using the word 'Nowell', which comes from the same collection, runs like this:

The child this day is born
A child of high renown
Most worthy of a sceptre
A sceptre and a crown.
Nowell, Nowell, Nowell
Nowell sing all we may
Because the King of all kings
Was born this blessed day.

The French version of the carol has a chorus that runs:

Noël, Noël, Noël, Noël
Jesus est né, chantons Noël.

However, its opening verse starts with the words, '*Aujourd'hui le Roi des cieux*' ('Today the king of heaven'), which is quite different.

Despite these many unknowns, we can say with some certainty that 'The first Nowell' is sung to a traditional English folk melody, probably dating from the 17th century.

UNPACKING THE BIBLICAL STORY OF THE CAROL

This carol invites us to focus on the outsiders who come to Jesus and with whom we unite in worship.

Christmas (Noël) with its good news (nowells) comes first to outsiders—the shepherds on the cold hillside and the faraway wise men. Outsiders are drawn to Jesus, and Israel's king attracts worldwide interest. He becomes our heavenly Lord. He is for all: rich and poor, outsiders and insiders. Israel's king is Jesus (verse 2) who is Christ (verse 4), the child from earth and the rescuer from heaven whose death ('blood' in verse 4) will pay the price to bring us all home. We are likened to kidnap victims who need to be ransomed.

In this carol we sing 'Nowell': Christmas news! It is, indeed, Christmas headlines!

UNPACKING THE MEANING OF THE CAROL

In verse 1 we sing of the unexpected witnesses. The shepherds were wrapped up for the night, perhaps already under their blankets. The carol says that they lay keeping their sheep. Perhaps they lay across the sheepfold's entrance, as was the custom, forming the 'door' with their bodies. They were all tucked up for the night and they had no plans to 'go into town', where they were probably unwelcome anyway. Perhaps these shepherds wouldn't even have figured in the Roman census records: they were non-persons. But God sees things differently. To God they really did matter. Many others might have been witnesses, invited to the birth, but God chose those who least expected to be there. The last became the first.

In verses 3 and 4, the unexpected visitors are the wise men, stargazers drawn by a curiosity in the sky. They must have been very convinced of its prophetic significance to undertake such a long journey. It seems that God inspired a hunger and curiosity in them that drove them on. There were surely many other, much more local astrologers who must have noticed the phenomenon, but God drew these definite outsiders in, to be unexpected witnesses to the incarnation. This 'nowell', this Christmas news, is for those who come from the ends of the earth, those who are outsiders to Israel and probably even outsiders to the known world of that day.

In verse 5 we sing of the unexpected gifts. Even the traditional gifts of gold, frankincense and myrrh are out of place, 'outsiders', in this humble homestead near Bethlehem. They belong in a palace or a temple or an exotic medicine chest. It seems that this baby is going to displace everything in our world (or, rather, return everything to its rightful place). The poor end up with riches, and riches now appear in the poorest of surroundings.

Finally, in verse 6 the carol suddenly invites us all to join unexpected company. This baby is the great leveller. The poor unwelcome herdsmen and the wealthy foreign stargazers find themselves united in worship and are invited to join with us, whoever we are—we who sing this carol. Christ has already begun to put everything back as it should be in his great rescue plan. This plan will involve his death in a great exchange that is beyond our understanding, but whose outcome is crystal clear—namely a world made new, where outsiders are brought in, the last made first and strangers united as fellow worshippers focused on Jesus. By inviting outsiders in, God turns everything inside out.

BIBLE LINKS

On one level, the carol tells the story of the shepherds in Luke 2:8–20 and the story of the wise men in Matthew 2:1–12. At a deeper level, however, it tells the story of the outsider and welcomes those on the outside into the light of God's presence. Jesus' life and ministry are picked up in this carol. He is the one who turns everything inside out, eating with outcasts, teaching that the first will be last and that outsiders are to be welcomed into our homes. In his life, Jesus demonstrates that our God is Father to the fatherless and protector of the widow and orphan. In his death, he bought our freedom through his blood.

God made heaven and earth; he created the sea and everything else. God always keeps his word. He gives justice to the poor and food to the hungry. The Lord sets prisoners free and heals blind eyes. He gives a helping hand to everyone who falls. The Lord loves good people and looks after strangers. He defends the rights of orphans and widows, but destroys the wicked. The Lord God of Zion will rule for ever! Shout praises to the Lord!
PSALM 146:6–10

The Spirit of the Lord God has taken control of me! The Lord has chosen and sent me to tell the oppressed the good news, to heal the brokenhearted, and to announce freedom for prisoners and captives.
ISAIAH 61:1

Jesus closed the book, then handed it back to the man in charge and sat down. Everyone in the meeting place looked straight at Jesus. Then Jesus said to them, 'What you have just heard me read has come true today.'
LUKE 4:20–21

'The Son of Man came to look for and to save people who are lost.'
LUKE 19:10

Jesus then said, 'So it is. Everyone who is now first will be last, and everyone who is last will be first.'
MATTHEW 20:16

We three kings

GLOBAL CHRISTMAS

UNPACKING THE STORY BEHIND THE CAROL

While we have no idea of the creative strains and stresses involved in the composition of this carol, the story behind it is quite simple. The Revd John Henry Hopkins Junior, Rector of Christ's Church, Williamsport, Pennsylvania, wrote it in 1857 either to feature as part of a Christmas pageant at the General Theological Seminary in New York or as a Christmas present for his nephews and nieces in Vermont. As well as being a clergyman, John Hopkins was a writer, editor, illustrator and designer of stained-glass windows.

The legends that have grown up around the 'three kings' stem largely from the 14th-century writer Johannes de Hildenheim, a Carmelite monk who wrote the *Historia Trium Regum* ('The story of the three kings'). His story tells how the kings travel separately from different countries and meet near Jerusalem, how they worship the child and give him particular gifts, such as a golden apple and 30 pieces of gold, how they travel home, eventually die and are buried together, then how their relics are brought to Köln (Cologne) where they are supposed to be buried in the Shrine of the Three Kings in Cologne Cathedral. Matthew's account is far less embellished (see Matthew 2:1–12).

UNPACKING THE BIBLICAL STORY OF THE CAROL

The wise men or 'three kings' saw a new star in the east, which they understood to mean that a great king had been born in the kingdom of Israel. They travelled to see him, stopping in Jerusalem en route to find out where the Messiah was to be born. On discovering from King Herod that the scriptures stated that the Messiah would be born in Bethlehem, they journeyed there, promising to let Herod know where the child was. They found Jesus and Mary by following the star, went into the house, threw themselves on the ground before Jesus, worshipped him and gave him gifts of gold, frank-incense and myrrh. Then, after being warned in a dream not to go back to Herod, they returned to their country by a different route.

UNPACKING THE MEANING OF THE CAROL

This carol is a depiction of the journey of the wise men. In the first verse, they describe their journey across different terrains (reminiscent of Johannes de Hildenheim's account). The chorus reminds us of the star they saw in the east, which eventually showed them the way to Bethlehem. In the middle three verses, the wise men each separately describe the gifts they are bringing to Jesus and the symbolic meaning of those gifts: gold for a king, frankincense for a god and myrrh for embalming a body. The final verse looks forward to Jesus' second coming, when he arises in glory, fulfilling his role as king, God and Saviour, to acclaim from both earth and heaven.

There is no hint in Matthew's Gospel that the wise men actually followed 'yonder star' for the whole journey to Jerusalem in anything other than a metaphorical sense. They saw his star while they were in the east, so it certainly was their motivation for the journey; they saw it again over the place where the child was in Bethlehem, but it is hard to see how they could have used that particular star as a guide on the entire journey.

The carol describes the travellers as 'three kings', which has helped to perpetuate the myth that there were three of them and that they were kings. Johannes de Hildenheim gives us three figures, even naming them Melchior, Caspar and Balthazar, and gives their countries of origin. There are certainly three gifts mentioned in Matthew's Gospel, but there could have been more wise men, or even just two.

The other term used for the wise men is 'magi', who were wise people—not necessarily men. They were astrologers, astronomers or interpreters of signs, perhaps Zoroastrians. They were so learned that people called them 'magicians' (our word 'magic' comes from the same source as 'magi'). There is nothing in Matthew to suggest that they were 'kings', although they must have been wealthy to have brought such precious gifts and to have made the long, costly journey.

The rhythm of 'We three kings' evokes the plodding journey of the wise men: it is easy to imagine camels' feet coming down heavily on the downbeats. The verses also have a solemn majesty in their minor key, while the chorus lightens appropriately as they look up to the star and its bright wonder, lifting them above the tribulations of their heavy journey and the weighty significance of the gifts they carry.

BIBLE LINKS

The story of the wise men is told in Matthew 2:1–12, and the theme of kingship can be found from early in the Old Testament, when the people ask God for a king in 1 Samuel 8. David is seen as the ideal of kingship and Jesus is a king in David's line. The arrival of the wise men certainly brings political upheaval, as the king of the Jews, Herod, feels his throne threatened and orders a massacre to try to destroy the threat to his kingship. The theme of Jesus' kingship continues throughout his life, as the people try to make him king

(John 6:15), right up to the confrontation with Herod's son in Jesus' final week and the 'coronation' with the mocking crown of thorns.

Links have been made between the star of Bethlehem and Balaam's prophecy in Numbers 24:17: 'But some day, a king of Israel will appear like a star'. Perhaps there is an echo, too, of Isaiah's prophecy in Isaiah 60:3: 'Nations and kings will come to the light of your dawning day'. Certainly Simeon saw that Jesus' job was to do what Israel could not and to draw other nations to his light: 'With my own eyes I have seen what you have done to save your people, and foreign nations will also see this. Your mighty power is a light for all nations, and it will bring honour to your people Israel' (Luke 2:30–32).

While shepherds watched

GOOD NEWS OF PEACE

UNPACKING THE STORY BEHIND THE CAROL

This popular hymn is part of the post-reformation tradition. A large number of hymns were composed for congregational singing, notably in the Lutheran churches in Germany. The English tradition was, however, influenced by the Calvinist reformers, who permitted singing only to biblical texts, mostly psalms. The first complete English Psalter was produced by John Day in 1562 and consisted of all the psalms and some passages from the English Prayer Book. This remained the authorized Psalter in the Church of England until Nahum Tate and Nicolas Brady produced a new and expanded edition in 1696, which, among other biblical items, added this metrical version of Luke 2:8–14 to their collection.

This carol's popularity is also clear because it has been sung to over 100 different melodies. The British favourite version is called 'Winchester Old' and first appeared in Este's Psalter of 1592. Another popular melody is called 'Cranbrook', developed from the folk song 'On Ilkley Moor baht' 'at', in which the parallel pastoral setting is perhaps more than coincidental.

UNPACKING THE BIBLICAL STORY OF THE CAROL

'While shepherds watched' must surely be one of the nation's favourite carols. The words are well known even among those who don't go to church—witness the parodies about 'washing socks' and 'syrup spoon'! It is a song of good news, whose climax comes in the last verse with the angels' message of 'peace on earth'. The pastoral setting among ordinary people, the surprise angel visitation and the promise of hope seem to attract a sympathetic ear at this Christmas season, quite independently of the carol's scriptural content.

Almost the whole carol is caught up with the angels' appearance and their words to the shepherds on that Judean hillside. In fact, one of this carol's alternative titles is 'The vision of the shepherds'. Just like them, we are caught up in the wonder of it all.

UNPACKING THE MEANING OF THE CAROL

The 18th-century language of the carol is not without its problems for 21st-century congregations. For example, what is a 'seraph'? The term 'swathing' is equally obscure and the words 'tidings', 'forthwith', 'throng' and 'mighty dread' are not very enlightening for some people, particularly children. Just in case you are already wondering, 'seraph' is the singular of seraphim (as in cherubim and seraphim), who are celestial beings of the highest order: that is to say, they are top-ranking angels.

Whenever angels appear in the Bible, they almost always have to say to us poor humans, 'Fear not!' This suggests that angels are far from the gentle, feathery folk that some portrayals would have us believe. Rather, they seem to be beings who frighten the living daylights out of those they visit. In the context of this carol, 'mighty dread' may be archaic, but it does capture the shepherds' real sense of shock.

The child 'of David's line' is Jesus and he was 'born a saviour'. His act of rescue or saving is the source of the peace about which the angels sing in the last verse. That promise of 'peace on earth and good will toward men' can be a puzzle to contemporary ears.

Clearly, since Jesus' birth in the world, there have still been an abundance of wars and ill will of all sorts. So what did the angels mean? Perhaps they are saying that this Christmas baby offers a completely new kind of peace and good will. Although we can refuse this offer (and, sadly, have done), all is not lost. The glory of God, and his 'kindness and truth' have appeared in Jesus (John 1:14) and are gifts waiting to be received, just as 'the peace that no one can completely understand' is now possible because Jesus has made peace by his death on the cross. The will to do good and not evil is also available through the gift of the Spirit of Christ, who lives in our hearts. In this sense, here is a baby who can change everything, and these are the 'glad tidings of great joy' about which the angels sing.

BIBLE LINKS

The Bible background to the story of this carol is found in Luke 2:8–14, which describes the third of four angel visitations that Luke records in his story of Christmas. Put together with these, the carol underlines the unique moment of history that the incarnation represents. It highlights the spiritual collision of temporal and eternal, as the veil between earth and heaven is pulled back and God's messengers pass through.

Encounters with angels in the Bible are often full of mystery and a good deal of terror. Abraham entertains three angel visitors in the desert (Genesis 18:1–15), Joshua meets with a warrior angel (Joshua 5:13–15), Samson's mother has an encounter with an angel (Judges 13:2–7), an angel described as being 'like a god' walks with Daniel's three friends in the fiery furnace (Daniel 3:21–25), and even Balaam's donkey is startled by the sight of an angel, with quite remarkable results (Numbers 22:22–35).

The appearance of angels to shepherds does have some Old Testament precedent. Moses was working as a shepherd when he encountered the presence of God and heard a voice speaking out of the flames of a bush. Angel messengers are described as 'flaming fire' in Hebrews 1:7, and the awe and wonder of Moses' experience in the desert is picked up in the terror felt by the shepherds on the hillside outside Bethlehem as they are told about the baby who would change everything.

Shepherds did not rank high in the social fabric of those days, and the fact that angels should appear to shepherds at their work, rather than to high-ranking Jewish leaders, must have surprised early Jewish Christian readers of this story. Something unusual must certainly have been happening. However, the choice of shepherds was not accidental. The leaders of God's people are called shepherds of the flock of Israel, and the prophet Ezekiel in particular takes them to task for how badly they have done their job (Ezekiel 34:1–6). By contrast, Ezekiel then goes on to talk about the coming of a true shepherd one day, who will go to great pains to rescue his flock (vv. 11–30). This is the very child whom the shepherds of this carol come to see in the manger. These shepherds come face-to-face with *the* good shepherd who will one day lay down his life for the sheep (John 10:15).

Part Three

USING A BIBLE*LANDS* PROJECT
RELATED TO THE CAROLS

For more information about the work of Bible*Lands*, together with a
downloadable PowerPoint Presentation of images relating to the
projects in this section, please go to www.biblelands.org.uk.

*

BIBLE*LANDS* PROJECTS

Here are some of the projects supported by Bible*Lands*, which could be presented as part of your carol service to illustrate the relevant theme.

AWAY IN A MANGER

Themes: Homes and belonging

JL Schneller School, Bekaa Valley, Lebanon

The Schneller School provides an education for 500 children aged from five to 18 years. The story of Schneller School goes back to 1860, when a German pastor named Johann Ludwig Schneller gave ten orphans a home in Jerusalem during the persecution of Christians in Lebanon. Johann's grandson moved the school to its current location in 1952.

For some of the children, without a family or from deprived circumstances, the school is also a home for them. There are boarding facilities for around 170 boys and, in more recent years, Bible*Lands* provided funding to enable 27 girls to board at the school for the first time. During the Lebanese conflict of 2006, Schneller School also provided a safe shelter for 150 displaced people who were made homeless for several months during the conflict.

GOD REST YOU MERRY, GENTLEMEN

Themes: Hope, good news and light out of darkness

Helen Keller Centre for the Visually Impaired, Jerusalem

The Helen Keller Centre for the Visually Impaired provides education and care for around 60 boys and girls with visual impairment, including 20 boarders, aged three to twelve years. Originally founded by English missionary Mary Lovell in the 1890s, it was the first school for blind children in Palestine. Today it has gained a reputation as a highly regarded centre of excellence in the care and development of young people with visual impairment.

The centre teaches all the usual curricular subjects, including Arabic Braille. As the children become older, they learn to use specialized equipment that provides them with additional skills to help their education. Students are also given training in mobility, orientation and daily living skills to enhance their independence. As they leave the centre to attend mainstream schools, the centre continues to support the students wherever possible, helping them to integrate into society and to lead fulfilled, educated lives.

GOOD KING WENCESLAS

Themes: Good will and caring for others in need

The Salaam Centre for Medico-Social Services (SCMSS), Cairo

The Salaam Centre for Medico-Social Services (SCMSS) is situated on the outskirts of Cairo. It provides health care and emergency medical aid to those living amid the rubbish of the city in the most deprived urban living conditions imaginable. Here, people live in poverty and squalor on a rubbish tip, where they earn their meagre living by sorting through the rubbish brought in for recycling from Greater Cairo.

The centre was established in 1976 by nuns who rented a small hut in the centre of the rubbish tip in response to a desperate need for health care. Today, the Salaam Centre is a haven of peace to the surrounding community, providing primary health care and emergency medical aid to the poor people of the area. The three main areas of activity are a hospital and clinic facility, a child health care programme, and a school for children with disabilities.

HARK! THE HERALD-ANGELS SING

Themes: Light and life

St John Ophthalmic Hospital, Jerusalem

The St John Ophthalmic Hospital was opened in 1882 in Jerusalem. Today it provides essential treatment to thousands of Palestinians suffering from serious eye conditions. The hospital has 80 beds, with an international team of surgeons and a staff of over 100, and treats nearly 40,000 patients each year. It helps in both restoring sight and maintaining vision for those suffering from eye disease or injury.

It also treats a further 44,000 people through its mobile outreach clinics to more remote villages in the West Bank. Three additional static clinics in the West Bank provide eye care to those who are unable to get to the St John Ophthalmic Hospital due to current travel restrictions.

Treatment is entirely free for the young and those who cannot afford to pay.

O COME, ALL YE FAITHFUL

Themes: Refugees and rebuilding shattered lives

Refuge Egypt and St Andrew's Refugee Ministry, Cairo

Refuge Egypt and St Andrew's Refugee Ministry are two projects working with refugees in Cairo. Refuge Egypt provides care and assistance to refugees from Sudan, Somalia and Eritrea who have just arrived in Cairo, many having lost everything, including homes and families. The traumatized refugees arrive into Egypt's already hugely overcrowded capital to an unfamiliar and sometimes hostile culture. Refuge Egypt provides emergency food, clothing and health care to meet their most urgent needs. Without refugee status, this community has no access to medical care or other vital services, and Refuge Egypt provides assistance with advocacy and support in registering for refugee status. It also provides education, training and employment, and help with repatriation and resettlement.

St Andrew's Refugee Ministry works alongside Refuge Egypt to help refugees rebuild their future by providing education for children and vocational training for adults. It also helps these displaced people to develop the handicraft skills they have brought with them, to help them find employment. Many of the staff are themselves from the refugee community.

O LITTLE TOWN OF BETHLEHEM

Theme: Refuge in Bethlehem

The Sheepfold, Bethlehem

In the Middle East, there is very little provision for children with disability. In response to this need, Mary Rewers set up a day centre in 1991 for children in Bethlehem who are so severely disabled that other institutions are unable to help them. Today, The Sheepfold can accommodate about 15 children, either as residential or day students. It aims to give each child the vital opportunity to develop their God-given potential. By showing them that they are loved, valued and accepted individuals who are precious in God's sight, it also helps them to develop a sense of self-worth. Without The Sheepfold, many of these children would have no real quality of life.

ONCE IN ROYAL DAVID'S CITY

Themes: Care for children and those who live in poverty

DUET, Upper Egypt

The Development of Upper Egypt Trust (DUET) is a small organization that makes a big difference. Many communities in the villages of Upper Egypt live in extreme poverty, in cramped, un-hygienic conditions, suffering from malnutrition and often disease. Illiteracy and general lack of education and training make it impossible for these people to improve their situation. DUET works in partnership with Village Development Committees to bring about valuable changes in these communities. Through small-scale projects in individual villages, such as primary health care, income generation, education and agricultural training, it enables these communities to break out of the cycle of poverty and look forward to the future with hope.

SILENT NIGHT

Themes: Peace and grace

Four Homes of Mercy, Bethany

The Four Homes of Mercy was founded in 1940 as a result of one woman's vision to care for destitute people. It is the only residential care home of its kind in the Palestinian Territories and provides shelter and care for 90 children and adults with severe disabilities, mainly from very poor backgrounds, who are some of the most vulnerable people in the community. Through rehabilitation and a variety of activities, each individual at the home is encouraged to have a sense of self-worth and well-being. A vocational training programme gives residents the opportunity to learn practical skills such as cookery and woodwork. In 2006 a 'peace garden' was opened, providing residents with a place not only to relax but also to enjoy the great satisfaction of growing their own plants.

THE FIRST NOWELL

Themes: Welcoming others, and the unexpected

The Spafford Children's Centre, Jerusalem

The Spafford Children's Centre began in 1925 when Bertha Spafford Vester took care of a young baby in Jerusalem whose mother had died and whose father was unable to look after the child. As she took more babies into her care, her home became known as the Spafford Baby Home. Today the Spafford Centre provides a range of services in medical, educational and social care for many disadvantaged children from the local community and the West Bank.

For young people living in the current climate of instability and conflict, the centre provides a range of activities to help them develop both mentally and socially in areas such as art, drama and dance. As it adapts and changes to the needs of the local community, the centre provides a place of refuge in troubled times.

WE THREE KINGS

Theme: Journeys

Rawdat El-Zuhur School, Jerusalem

Rawdat El-Zuhur School was founded in 1952 as a home for destitute girls. Responding to the changing needs of the community, the home became a school for both boys and girls and today educates around 250 children between the ages of four and twelve. The children, who are mostly Muslim, come from very poor families, with whom the school works hard to develop good relationships.

Many of the children at Rawdat El-Zuhur School face long, stressful and sometimes impossible journeys to and from their place of study, as a consequence of travel restrictions caused by checkpoints and the separation wall. To help these young people cope with the situation, the school arranges special activities throughout the year and encourages free expression through an emphasis on music, dance, art, drama and sport. At this popular school, children are keen to get to their lessons and there is a waiting list of those eagerly hoping for a place.

WHILE SHEPHERDS WATCHED

Themes: Peace and service

Nazareth School of Nursing

The Nazareth School of Nursing was founded in 1924 as part of the ministry of the Nazareth Hospital. Currently there are about 200 nurses in training and entry to the school is open to all, without any racial, ethnic or religious constraints or prejudice. It is the only nursing school available to Arab students in the whole of Israel, where Christian, Muslim and Jew learn alongside each other and classes are given in English, Hebrew and Arabic. Although it is a multi-faith school, students are trained in a Christian environment, and ethics, for example, are taught from a Christian standpoint. After training, the nurses serve in hospitals and medical centres throughout the country, and it is said that there is hardly a village in Galilee that does not have a Nazareth-trained nurse.

Part Four

INVOLVING CHILDREN
IN A CREATIVE CAROL SERVICE

*

CREATIVE IDEAS
FOR EXPLORING THE CAROLS

The first nativity

St Francis of Assisi is well known as the patron saint of animals and founder of the Franciscan monastic order. Around the year 1220, he celebrated Christmas by setting up the first nativity crib in the town of Greccio, near Assisi. He used real animals to create the nativity scene so that worshippers could contemplate the birth of Jesus in a direct way.

With this in mind, encourage people to think about the visual aids that might have been present at the first Christmas. Have the following items to help spark the imagination.

- A small bag of fresh hay
- A small bottle of water and a shallow bowl
- A baby's shawl or blanket
- A soft toy animal (preferably a cow, sheep or donkey)
- Glow stars, or stars cut from holographic paper

Hide the visual aids in different parts of the worship space and, before the singing of the carol, choose a few of the children to hunt out the hidden items. When all the items have been found, read the words of Luke 2:7: '[Mary] gave birth to her firstborn son. She dressed him in baby clothes and laid him on a bed of hay, because there was no room for them in the inn.'

Next, ask the children which of the items would definitely have been present at the first Christmas and which wouldn't. Point out that although water is not mentioned in the nativity story in the Bible, it is very important to our well-being. Ask in what ways water might have been needed on that first Christmas night. We associate animals such as cattle, sheep and donkeys with the nativity story, but no creatures are mentioned in the biblical story. In what ways would the nativity story be different if we didn't include the animals?

Finally, think about the night sky and the vastness of God's creation. Stars are traditionally associated with the Christmas stories. Why is this? Stars are millions of light years away. Their light has travelled for many, many years before we see it shining in the night sky. It is amazing to think that the stars that lit the night sky at the beginning of creation are possibly the very ones seen at Jesus' birth, and visible to our eyes today. Imagine the stars mentioned in the carol being flung into space at the very start of creation. They were created by the hand of God and, in the imagery of this carol, are now looking at their maker—a tiny baby asleep on a bed of hay. You might like to consider darkening the worship space and projecting images of star clusters, such as the Milky Way or the Pleiades cluster, on to a screen or wall while the carol is being sung. Star images can be downloaded from the Internet on to a laptop for a PowerPoint display, or transferred to acetate for use with an OHP.

GOD REST YOU MERRY, GENTLEMEN

A Victorian Christmas

This carol draws us towards the nostalgia of Christmas celebrations over a hundred years ago and reminds us that, through the years, the Christmas message has remained the same, passed on from generation to generation.

Many towns and villages hold a Victorian evening at Christmas, providing the opportunity to build community and create a pleasant environment for 'out of hours' Christmas shopping. If there is such an evening planned for your locality, you could consider continuing the theme in your carol service, thus providing a bridge between the life of the local church and the people of the local community, some of whom may rarely come to church except at Christmas.

You could create a traditional atmosphere by paying special attention to the way the worship space is decorated. Use traditional holly, ivy and evergreens to decorate pillars and windowsills. Decorate the Christmas tree with traditional tinsel (very popular in Victorian times), silver wire ornaments, sugar candy sticks and glass beads. Perhaps you could run some all-age craft sessions during Advent to make typical Victorian decorations, such as snowflakes and stars, or paper baskets filled with sugared sweets. Fixing small candles on to the tree with wire holders was also popular in Victorian times. However, towards the end of the 19th century, trees began to be decorated with electric lights, which were patented in 1882. Glass baubles were also popular in Victorian times (nowadays, non-glass are safer).

Christmas cards and crackers were both Victorian inventions. The idea for Christmas cards was borrowed from Valentine's Day, allowing people to send love and good wishes to each other at Christmas without romantic overtones. Pictures of children and angels were popular. You may like to consider setting up some all-age workshops to research and create homemade Victorian-style Christmas card and cracker designs to incorporate into the decoration of the worship space for your carol service. If you plan to make Christmas cards, they could be given to members of your community once the service is over.

Many Victorian evenings include traditional Victorian dress and you may be able to enhance the theme further by borrowing costumes for those taking part in the service. You could also provide paper lanterns for the children to hold and have Victorian fare such as small slices of plum pudding or mince pies and warm, spicy fruit punch after the service.

GOOD KING WENCESLAS

What happens next?

Strictly speaking, this carol doesn't really belong within the flow of a carol service that is telling the biblical story, but, because of its popularity and familiarity to outsiders, it is well worth including. It would probably be best to place it near the end, where it could naturally invite us to respond to the question 'What happens next?'

The life of Jesus began in the stable but ended in the story of the cross and resurrection. It is Jesus' life, death and resurrection that inspired Christian saints like Stephen and Wenceslas—and Agnes, too, for that matter. One way to illustrate the link between this St Stephen's Day carol and the cross could be as follows.

Set up a series of simple visuals in one area of the worship space (preferably at the front), based on items from the traditional Christmas story, but within which the cross is somewhere visible. For example:

- The 'X' shape beneath the traditional manger.
- The cross shape within the star.
- The cross shapes caught in the timbers of the stable.
- The shape of Mary holding a baby in her arms, casting the shadow of a cross on the ground.
- The crosses that may traditionally have adorned the wise men's crowns.

Although few people realized it at the time, the cross was part of the crib scene because it would be only through death that lasting new life could come into the world. Additional cross shapes could be hidden for the children to come and find. Disguise them among traditional Christmas symbols such as the decorations, cards, wrapping paper, holly and so on. This underlines the carol's message that there is something more to Christmas than tinsel and turkey.

Christmas giveaway

The emphasis on kindness and caring for others in this carol could be explored by using it as an opportunity to focus the service at this point on a 'Christmas giveaway' rather than the usual Christmas indulgence. Children and adults could be asked to buy an extra present during the weeks of Advent, some additional festive food and a second set of Christmas decorations, which they could then bring to the service. In the course of the carol, when the page is asked to bring food, wine and pine logs, people could be invited to bring their giveaway items to a predesignated area. This invitation could be made while an extra instrumental verse is played. You might also wish to consider setting up a simple replica of a St Agnes' fountain.

This might also be a good moment to bring to the front any money collected for BibleLands. The page could then collect some of the items from the pile to carry as he or she mimes the final verses of the carol in the footsteps of the king. The items collected could later become a gift to a local hospital, hospice or night shelter, or sold at auction for BibleLands.

HARK! THE HERALD-ANGELS SING

Angels on beanpoles

During the singing of 'Hark! the herald-angels sing', you could hold a simple angel procession. For this you will need angels on beanpoles, which can be prepared before the service. Prepare as many angels as you can.

Scale up an angel shape to make a template about a metre long. (You should be able to find a simple angel outline on the Internet or on a Christmas card, or you could use the template on page 210.) Using your template, cut out angel outlines from white or gold card and decorate them with glitter, gold and silver 'icicles' and holographic foil shapes. Mount the angels on beanpoles using sticky tape. The poles can also be decorated with giftwrapping ribbon or foil.

Just before the carol, read Luke 2:8–14. If possible, display or project an image of a very humble, grubby manger and baby to depict the theme of 'laying his glory by' and becoming one of us. During each verse, while the carol is sung, the angels can be held at head height and, during the chorus, they can be lifted as high as they can go.

- **Verse 1**: Angels process through the centre of the congregation and stand spread out down the nave or aisle.
- **Verse 2**: Angels walk forward to meet facing the congregation at the front of the worship space.
- **Verse 3**: Angels spread around the outside of the congregation, encircling it.

O COME, ALL YE FAITHFUL

A crescendo of invitation

The repeated chorus in this carol makes it memorable and approachable for children and early learners, even though the content of some of the verses may perhaps be too complex for them (and perhaps for adults, too!).

Many congregations and choirs encourage different groups of singers to sing the successive lines of 'O come, let us adore him', building up each time to a climax with everyone singing. Some of these choruses could be given to children's groups to create their own crescendo of invitation, starting with the youngest for the first line, adding the middle juniors for the second and then all the children and young people together for line three.

If the children sing all the choruses in this way (with the possible exception of the last one), then the adults can divide up some of the other verses, perhaps women singing verse 2 and men singing verse 3. Everyone sings the last verse together.

O LITTLE TOWN OF BETHLEHEM

Visualizing the carol

This is a very atmospheric carol with strong images. If it is sung by a children's choir, as was the original intention in Philadelphia, it can be a very powerful part of a carol service and could be accompanied by a series of visuals projected on to a screen. You could use some pictures from the National Gallery website (www.nationalgallery.org.uk) or elsewhere on the Internet, or perhaps enlarged postcard art pictures of appropriate paintings (also available from the National Gallery). Suggested images include:

Verse 1: Stillness and light

- A silhouette of Bethlehem beneath the stars
- Streetlights on a small back road
- A single candlelight

Verse 2: Sleeping and singing

- The picture *Nativity, at Night* by Geertgen tot Sint Jans, which shows many tiny angels hovering around the crib in gentle stillness
- An image of the night sky, filled with stars

Verse 3: Silence and prayer

- A picture of a person, kneeling in prayer

Verse 4: Triumphant arrival

- A picture of Christ in glory
- Angels dancing and celebrating around a nativity scene as in *The Mystic Nativity* by Botticelli

ONCE IN ROYAL DAVID'S CITY

Riches and rags

For a themed Christmas service on the contrast between wealth and poverty, you could decorate half the worship space or stage area with sumptuous fabrics and furniture, luxurious foods and bottles of wine, expensive tasteful party decorations, even going so far as having willing volunteers to act as servants, waiters, beauticians, personal trainers and similar 'millionaire's staff'. The other half of your chosen area can be decorated with wheelie bins, cardboard boxes, empty beer bottles, litter and, if desired, willing volunteers to be down-and-outs, refugees, street children and so on. Refer to the contrast at different points through the service, or have a running improvised sketch, showing attempts to persuade the millionaire on one side to leave his or her area and join the people on the other side.

This visual contrast might also be the focus for a reflection on where God might be found today on earth—among the rich or among the poor?

Poverty through art

Picking up on the theme of the second verse of the carol, explore through art the idea of God coming to live with those in poverty. Supply paper, collage materials and paints or crayons and prepare a display of the artwork produced.

Our childhood's pattern

An alternative theme in this carol is that of Jesus being 'our childhood's pattern'. Give out an outline of a child on graph paper or squared paper and ask adults and children to design patterns that might symbolize the perfect childhood of Jesus. What colours might you use for different moods? What shapes might represent different behaviour or actions or events? Use these colours and shapes to fill the outline of the child.

You could extend this activity by filling in the outline of a second child, one more like us, where the patterns aren't perfect and the shapes go wrong. Then display the perfect and the imperfect side by side. How wonderful that our perfect God loves us with all our difficult bits!

SILENT NIGHT

The nativity at night

Display *The Nativity at Night* by Geertgen tot Sint Jans (downloadable from www.nationalgallery.org.uk) and ask some of the following questions:

- What colours do you think of as 'Christmassy' colours?
- What colours has the artist used in this picture of Christmas?
- What time of day is this picture set, do you think? How can you tell?
- Why do you think Jesus was born at night?
- Where is the light coming from?
- Which characters can you see clearly?
- Which characters are in shadow but still visible?
- At what point in Luke's narrative do you think this story occurs?
- What might the artist be trying to say by showing angels around the manger?
- Look at Mary: what do you notice about her hands?
- What is Mary thinking?
- Look at the baby: what is he wearing?
- What is he lying on?
- What's unusual about this manger?
- How does the artist make you feel about the baby?
- What words would you use to describe the mood of the picture?
- How does the picture make you feel?
- When have you felt like that before?
- Is this scene anything like your experience of Christmas? If so, how? If not, why not?
- How might you find this peace and quietness at Christmas time?

The carol 'Silent night' was written 400 years after this picture was painted, but echoes some of the themes that the artist has included.

Read through the words of the carol again carefully. Which themes or ideas are the same in the carol and the picture? Which are different? Sing or listen to a recording of the carol with the picture still on display.

THE FIRST NOWELL

Party invitations

Develop the idea of the guests of honour at your carol service. Think what it would mean to invite an immigrant worker and a foreign ambassador as the chief guests, especially if, in so doing, you leave out the local mayor, the local police chief, or even the local clergy! God is reminding us for whom this birth is planned—not just for our close, comfortable circle of friends but for the full range of people within the bookends of his kingdom, including people such as migrants and foreign ministers.

Next, draw up a list of potential guests to invite to Jesus' birthday party. Along with Mary and Joseph (and the baby himself) we have first the relatives: Zechariah and Elizabeth and baby John. Next we have the kind innkeeper and his wife, perhaps some midwives and some of the other guests from the inn. Next come the stable boy, the farmer who owns the ox and the salesman who has stabled his donkey there for the night. Finally, there are the migrant workers who are doing the jobs that no one else will do (in this case, looking after the sheep on the cold hillside) and some wealthy foreign tourists whose curiosity has caused them to drop by.

Invite members of the congregation to fill each role as you call it out. Next, line everyone up for a 'group photo' and then debate who should be where in the photo. Plan it so that the migrant workers and tourists get pushed to the back. But then stop the scene (freeze it) and remind everyone that God's idea of the photo for this scene was completely different. Now everyone else, apart from the migrant workers and the tourists, is pushed to the back. It's a scandal! An outrage! An affront! It's God's inside-out incarnation!

Inside out

As a visual focus for the service, make some capes that are rough on the outside and rich and decorative on the inside for the shepherds, and some that are rich and decorative on the outside and rough on the inside for the wise men. When they arrive at the nativity scene, they should turn the capes inside out, so that the shepherds are now blessed with the riches of seeing Jesus and the wise men give up their riches in honour of Jesus.

Extend this idea using some simple bags with a sumptious fabric 'inside' and a jute 'outside'. Turn the bags inside out to show the change that Jesus brings. For the shepherds, a picture of a sheep could be on the rough outside and a picture of the nativity on the rich inside. For the wise men, there could be a star on the rich outside and a picture of the nativity on the rough inside.

Other contrasts include: poor becomes rich; far becomes near; last becomes first; unwanted becomes loved; unknown becomes welcomed; stranger becomes friend.

WE THREE KINGS

Global Christmas

The wise men came from different countries and cultures but still worshipped the same Jesus. Before the service, ask those attending to bring along any Christmas items they might have from other countries, such as nativity sets, cards, pictures, traditional food, music and so on, which could be displayed in the worship space to remind everyone of the worldwide family of faith. If the display is set up in a church, local schools might be very interested to see this exhibition.

Stained-glass decorations

You could echo the skills of this carol's creator by making themed stained-glass windows. Either use black card to form the frames and leading, and coloured tissue paper for the glass, or paint on to clear glass jam jars and place tealight candles inside them. Use shapes such as gifts, stars, crowns and simple outlines of travellers.

Tableaux

Bring the carol to life with three singing voices (there is no evidence that the three kings were all men—the term 'magi' can mean people of either sex, so you can use female voices, too). For each verse, make a tableau (a still picture), using the chorus to enter and exit the stage area. For example:

- **Verse 1:** A tableau of the journey, with the magi in different moods: one pointing hopefully forward, one tired out and lagging behind, one carrying all the baggage.
- **Verse 2:** A tableau of a crowned king sitting on a throne, with the first wise person holding out the gift.
- **Verse 3:** Borrow a thurible (incense burner) from a local church that uses incense. Invite someone to act as thurifer and swing the thurible gently, with the wise person kneeling, holding out the gift—not to the thurifer, but out to the front. Try to make the thurible the only moving thing in the tableau. If that is not practicable, use the suggestion in the 'Creative worship' section on page 184. Place the incense on charcoal in a large earthenware dish and watch the smoke rise, like prayers rising to God. (Psalm 141:2 says, 'Think of my prayer as sweet-smelling incense.')

- **Verse 4:** A tableau of a crucifixion. Have someone with their arms stretched out as if on a cross, with the wise person holding out the gift to him or her.
- **Final verse:** A tableau of the magi kneeling in front of Mary and Jesus, all holding out their gifts.

WHILE SHEPHERDS WATCHED

Creative voices

'While shepherds watched' contains a number of 'voices' and could be read or sung by different people accordingly. For example, verse 1 could be recited by a single voice (narrator). Verse 2 could be recited or sung by a narrator and someone representing the angel of the Lord. Verses 3 and 4 could be narrated or sung by the angel, verse 5 by a narrator and, finally, verse 6 by a group of angels and the angel of Lord.

God's own special lamb

The carol also lends itself to creative storytelling. For example:

What a commotion there was out on the Bethlehem hillside that night—bright lights, heavenly singing and that amazing message! God's special king had come. Everyone in those days knew that God's chosen Messiah was going to arrive one day, so the Bethlehem shepherds realized straightaway that this message was important.

History was coming to a turning point and mere shepherds were the first to know about it. They would be first with the news—what a scoop! Can you imagine their excitement, amazement and joy? They were more than likely just hired shepherds taking the night shift, but God had chosen to speak to them. Mind you, it was probably not by chance that God chose to go to shepherds first. Shepherds have always been very important to God, and the good shepherd had long been a picture of God's character.

So off they went to Bethlehem, running, dancing, tumbling and leaving their sheep. It must have been important—fancy leaving their livelihood behind! That would have been unheard of. And I wonder what the sheep thought of all this? Well, let's use our imaginations to find out.

First of all, imagine how puzzled the sheep must have looked! They certainly would have been upset to lose their shepherds. Who would feed and protect them? What should they do? There was no question about it: they would have to follow (a very predictable thing for sheep to do), so off they trotted down the hill.

In fact, the hill was so steep that they fell and almost flew down that slope. So much so that one local neighbour, who saw them tumbling past his window, was inspired to write the first Christmas carol. You know the one: 'I saw three *sheep* come *tumbling* by, on Christmas Day, on Christmas Day…'.

They arrived at the outskirts of the town. Where next? Where should they look for their shepherds? They hadn't really understood the angels' message, except that they had gathered that someone special was in town. So, if they found that someone, then perhaps they would find their masters.

Angels come from God, so off they went to the local synagogue, but no luck there. It was shut up, dark and empty. There was no one about.

Angels are important, so next they tried the town hall. But that was also shut up—closed for business until next Tuesday. Typical!

Perhaps this special person was a new leader of some sort. If so, perhaps he would be with the soldiers at the guard post. But the sheep had no luck there either. There were just a few centurions warming themselves by an open fire. No sign of any special visitor and no shepherds.

Where could they be? Where should they look next? They wandered about for a while like… like… like… well, like lost sheep!

Eventually they started to feel hungry and began to look around for some food. They left the main streets and went down the back alleys. All of a sudden, an old cattle shed caught their eye. It looked attractive; some lights were on and people were talking. They drew close and peeked in at the door, and guess what? There were their shepherds.

One sheep pushed in first and, when his master saw him, he picked him up and held him close to a straw-filled feeding trough. Ah, food at last! But no—there was a baby lying there.

The shepherd smiled and said, 'Look! You've not only found your shepherd, but also God's own special lamb.'

The sheep was rather puzzled, but he also felt privileged as he looked at his master and the baby. It seemed that, somehow, the three of them had a lot in common. 'Fancy God's special person being a tiny baby in a cattle shed,' he thought. 'What a surprise!'

*

IDEAS FOR EXPLORING
THE CAROLS THROUGH POETRY

AWAY IN A MANGER

The cost of love

Here is a poem that you could use to explore the message of
salvation underlying this carol.

> *There are too many noughts in the days of a star*
> *To measure its life and compare it with ours.*
> *Our eyes cannot see, our minds cannot grasp*
> *How something so small can be so very vast.*
>
> *Lord of creation, your hands made the stars,*
> *A myriad jewels in a light-filled dome.*
> *Our eyes cannot see, our minds cannot grasp*
> *The vastness of you, Lord, who made us your own.*
>
> *There are precious few years between crib and dust*
> *Yet you gave up heaven's grandeur to become one of us.*
> *Our eyes cannot see, our minds cannot grasp*
> *How much you surrendered to make eternity ours.*
>
> *Lord of creation, you came as a babe,*
> *A borrowed manger, a borrowed grave.*
> *Our eyes cannot see, our minds cannot grasp*
> *The cost of your love poured out on the cross.*

GOD REST YOU MERRY, GENTLEMEN

19th-century verse

Christmas was very much a family time in the 19th century. Typically, the Victorians would entertain themselves at home around a roaring fire, and poetry reading was a popular feature. You could incorporate a Victorian poem into your service. There are many to choose from with a Christmas theme, such as Gerard Manley Hopkins' 'Moonless darkness stands between' (*Oxford Poetry Library*, OUP, 1995) and Thomas Hardy's 'The oxen' (*The Illustrated Poets*, Aurum Press Ltd, 1990), both of which are suitable for adults and children alike. You may wish to use selected stanzas rather than the whole poem, intersperse the stanzas at different points in the service, or present the poem as a performance reading with children and adults taking part.

GOOD KING WENCESLAS

Pinchpence's doggerel

This carol helps turn our attention to the plight of those in need at Christmas. Within its words, there are faint Victorian echoes of another morality tale from this era, namely *A Christmas Carol* by Charles Dickens. In that story, Scrooge is woken out of his miserliness through a series of nightmares and becomes at last a paragon of generosity. Wenceslas needed no such dreams. He had already been moved to a selfless life by his commitment to Jesus Christ. But what if he hadn't become a Christian? How then might this carol have sounded? Here is a suggestion—but beware: this version contains even more heavy doggerel!

All: Greedy Pinchpence last looked out
      To the east one evening
      Headlines sad told all about
      War and trade uneven.
      Futures gone, it's just not right
      To lead a life most cruel.
      But when the needy came in sight,
      He showed no care at all.

Pinchpence: Turn the page; it's not for me,
      The misery they are selling.
      They're not poor—oh, can't you see?
      'Tis downright lies they're telling.
Page: Shame on you, you heartless man!
      You know your wealth is mounting.
      Hear their cry while you can,
      'Tis on your help they're counting.

Pinchpence: Bring me food and bring me wine
      And sofas made of leather.
      What I own I'll keep as mine.
      The poor? Why should I bother?
All: Appeals for help, ignored they were,
      Charities unheeded.
      What a world, it's so unfair.
      But this is what our greed did.

All: So, mark the Saviour's steps from God,
      Let those in need be given
      Even shares and not the odd
      By injustice driven.
      Therefore, Christians all, be sure,
      Grace and wealth possessing,
      If you should ignore the poor,
      You'll not get the blessing.

Word poems

The following idea will need some preparation with a group before the service. The key themes in the carol are the cold weather, the wealthy king, the poverty of the wood gatherer, and the example of Christian generosity set by Wenceslas for his page and us. Put simply, we have cold, poverty, wealth and kindness.

Invite a group to work together to find as many words as they can that are linked to each of these themes. They will find some in the carol. Build up a strong word collection, ready to introduce it. For example:

- **Cold:** snow, ice, freezing, bitter, chilly, shivering, frosty and biting wind
- **Poverty:** penniless, sad, starving, drab, dull, weak, helpless and vulnerable
- **Wealth:** rich, monied, secure, powerful, comfortable, cash-laden, well dressed and carefree
- **Kindness:** generous, thoughtful, caring, sensitive, alert, helpful, sacrificial, open-handed and giving

Now collect these words together to build up four 'word poems' to help set the scene for the carol. Each mini-poem should be made up of lines containing two words or phrases, with the shorter word first. You may even create some incidental rhythm and rhymes when doing this. For example:

> *Snowy and shivering*
> *Icy and quivering*
> *Chilly and wind biting*
> *Frosty and teeth-chattering*

Four groups could then each read out their poem in chorus, one after the other, to set the scene for the carol to come.

HARK! THE HERALD-ANGELS SING

The light of God

The poem below can be presented by four people as a dramatic reading to explore the correlation between the light of God present at creation and the light of God present in Jesus.

1: In the beginning God created the heavens and the earth.

2: The earth was barren with no form of life.

3 and 4: Barren.

2 and 3: Barren.

1: It was under a roaring ocean covered with darkness.

2 and 3: Darkness.

3 and 4: Darkness.

1: But!

2: But the Spirit.

3: But the Spirit of God.

4: But the Spirit of God was moving.

2: Moving.

3: Moving.

All: But the Spirit of God was moving over the waters.

2: Walking over the waters.

3: Calming the waters.

1: And God said, 'Let light shine!'

4: And light shone.

1: And God saw that it was good.

2: It was good.

3: It is good.

4: It will be good.

 Reproduced with permission from *Bethlehem Carols Unpacked* published by BRF 2008 (978 1 84101 534 7)
www.barnabasinchurches.org.uk

2: I move.
3: I speak.
4: I see.
2: Moving.
3: Speaking.
4: Seeing.
2: Speaking God.
3: Moving.
4: Speaking God.
2: Seeing.
3: Speaking God.
4: God of words.
2: Of conversation.
3: Of story.
4: Of history.
2: Of words.
3: Words.

1: In the beginning was the Word.
4: In the beginning.
1: In the beginning was the Word.
4: The Word was with God and was truly God.
1: From the beginning.
4: Before the world was, he was.

2: He was.
3: He is.
4: He will be.

1: Everything was created by him in heaven and on earth.
2, 3 and 4: He moves.
1: Everything, seen and unseen.

Reproduced with permission from *Bethlehem Carols Unpacked* published by BRF 2008 (978 1 84101 534 7)
www.barnabasinchurches.org.uk

2, 3 and 4: He sees.

1:   All things were created by him and for him.

2, 3 and 4: He moves.

1:   He was before all things and in him all things hold together.

2, 3 and 4: He sees.

1:   With this Word, God made all things.

2, 3 and 4: He speaks.

1:   Nothing was made without the Word.

2:   Without the Story.

3:   Without the Breath.

4:   Without the Song.

2:   The Story.

2:   The Breath.

2:   The Song.

2:   Story.

2:   Breath.

2:   Song.

1:   Everything that was made received its light from him.

2:   Receive this light.

2:   Receive this light.

1:   And his life gave light to everyone.

All: Shine!

2 and 3: Shine as a light.

2, 3 and 4: Shine as a light in the world.

1:   Shine as a light in the world, to the glory.

All: Shine as a light in the world, to the glory of God the Father. Amen.

O COME, ALL YE FAITHFUL

O come, let us adore him

The words of the verses, translated from the original Latin by John Wade, could be updated into more modern English and perhaps spoken by a child or group of children or leaders between the sung choruses. For example:

Verse 1

Here's the invitation to all believers:
Come close now, smile like winners.
Bethlehem's the place where we gather to see
God's baby Son, born for you and me—wow!

O come, let us adore him, O come, let us adore him,
O come, let us adore him, Christ the Lord!

Verse 2

God's wrapped up small, as small as a lamb,
Changed his cosmic light into the tiniest flame.
God, yes God, sleeps upon the hay.
The eternal God now has a birthday—wow!

O come, let us adore him...

Verse 3

This blows heaven's mind and the angels go wild
A-shouting and a-singing about the Christ-child.
They all join in with a chorus of praise:
God is amazing, in spectacular ways—wow!

O come, let us adore him...

Verse 4

Yo! Welcome Lord Jesus, baby so small,
Our saving God, come to bless us all.
You deserve our applause and all our love.
In baby clothes, we see God from above—wow!

O come, let us adore him…

This Christmas

Here is a Christmas poem, which also invites us to do something.

The census crowds were occupied
When God first breathed and tears he cried;
And for a world that's still in danger,
Won't you be his living manger—this Christmas?

A frightened girl, a worried spouse
Left on the streets, no room, no house;
And for a world that's still unsure,
Won't you be his human stall—this Christmas?

Nightshift workers, angel-driven,
See the join of the earth and heaven;
And for a world so full of woes,
Won't you be his swaddling clothes—this Christmas?

Far-travelled gold was a gift for him
Who came as our sacrifice for sin;
And for a world, so rich but poor,
Won't you be his bed of straw—this Christmas?

Hillside choirs sang out in chorus;
To sing again, they're waiting for us;
So, for a world that's tired and worn
Won't you be the place where he's born—this Christmas?

O LITTLE TOWN OF BETHLEHEM

While Bethlehem sleeps

Here's a simple version of the carol for younger children to rehearse and perform with appropriate actions.

Hush, hush, while Bethlehem sleeps,
God, as a baby, in he creeps.
Light for our darkness; peace for our hearts.
As angels are singing, our sadness departs.

ONCE IN ROYAL DAVID'S CITY

With us

Immanuel is a name given to Jesus in the book of Isaiah. It means 'God with us'. Present the following poem with one person reading the verse and everyone joining in with the two chorus lines. Talk about what it means to be a best friend to someone. You could make up your own verse, using the same rhyme and metre, showing what you value most about your best friend. Can you think of any times in Jesus' life when he was a best friend to the people round him?

Reader: A good friend knows just how it feels
When the world turns dark and grey.
He'll stand by you when you're lonely,
When the others run away.

All: And he feeleth for our sadness,
And he shareth in our gladness,

Reader: She'll be glad when you get good news,
Get a star or pass a test.
When you win the race she'll cheer you,
She'll be glad when you're the best.

All: And he feeleth for our sadness,
And he shareth in our gladness.

Reader: He'll be there at different ages,
Never too young or old for you.
He knows what it's like to grow up.
Where we go, he's been there too.

All: And he feeleth for our sadness,
And he shareth in our gladness.

Reader: Born a baby, born among us,
Lived among us, lives here still.
Friend who shares our joy and sadness,
God with us—Immanuel.

All: And he feeleth for our sadness,
And he shareth in our gladness.

 Reproduced with permission from *Creative Ideas for Carol Services* published by BRF 2008 (978 1 84101 534 7)
www.barnabasinchurches.org.uk

SILENT NIGHT

Night words

- Collect words that describe night time. Divide them into positive words and negative words. Write a poem personifying Night as someone you would welcome into your house.
- Write a fourth verse for the carol, evoking the night when the wise men arrived to see the young Jesus. (It may not have been night-time, of course, but this will be better suited to the rest of the carol.)
- Write a version of the carol that shows how noisy it might have been on the night of Jesus' birth. See the 'Silent night?' sketch below for some ideas. Begin: 'Noisiest night, holy night…'.
- Look at the picture from the activity on page 117 (*The Nativity at Night* by Geertgen tot Sint Jans) and write a short poem inspired by your favourite detail in the picture.

THE FIRST NOWELL

The bigger picture

The following poem would fit very well either before or after the singing of the carol.

> *An outside God steps down from above.*
> *Outside people are brought into his love.*
> *Jesus on the outside becomes Jesus of the heart.*
> *Welcome to the kingdom of our inside-out God.*

> *God from the outside is now Jesus in our heart*
> *And people on the outside in our lives have a part.*
> *Jesus on the outside becomes Jesus of the heart.*
> *Welcome to the kingdom of our inside-out God.*

WE THREE KINGS

Three gifts

For a simple activity, invite everyone to think about the three gifts brought by the wise men. What do they tell us about the wise men? What do they tell us about Jesus? What three gifts would *we* give Jesus, knowing far more about him than the wise men did when they set out on their journey? Why would we give him these particular gifts?

You could expand this activity by using the same rhyme and metre as 'We three kings' to write verses about each of these gifts.

Word journey

This idea is based on a word train. Start by saying a word associated with the wise men. Then ask someone to suggest a word associated with your word. Continue inviting members of the congregation to add a word, building a word list until you have about ten words or until the energy dissipates, then recite the word journey. What strange routes has the journey taken? The word journey can also be carried out in small groups, with a spokesperson from each group relating their ten words to the whole congregation after a given time. Each contribution could be read out in the form of a word journey 'poem'.

Picture poems

Choose a great picture of the wise men from modern or traditional art, from the Western tradition or from another tradition. What words or phrases come to mind as you reflect on the picture? Write them down and see if any of them suggest a poem or poetical piece.

Published poems

Some poems about the wise men include:

- T.S. Eliot: 'Journey of the magi' (*The Lion Christian Poetry Collection*, Lion Hudson plc)
- Sidney Godolphin: 'Lord, when the wise men came from far' (*The Lion Christian Poetry Collection*)
- Isaac Watts: 'Miracles at the birth of Christ' (*The New Oxford Book of Christian Verse*, Oxford Paperbacks)
- Christopher Smart: 'Hymn 3 Epiphany' (*The New Oxford Book of Christian Verse*)
- Kate McIlhagga: 'Christmastide' (*The Green Heart of the Snowdrop*, Wild Goose Publications)

WHILE SHEPHERDS WATCHED

Good news of peace

Paradoxically, the 'good news of peace' shattered the peace of that hillside above Bethlehem. The shepherds had to be startled and disturbed into action to search for the lasting peace that God was giving in the shape of a baby. Perhaps the story reminds us that this sort of true peace has to be looked for, perhaps in the most unlikely places, and that to find it we often need to be uncomfortably jolted out of our false sense of peace.

The shepherds had two surprises that night—first of all, the appearance of angels in the night sky, then the discovery of a poor family with their newborn son in a stable. No wonder, as the story says, the shepherds couldn't stop talking about it for days afterwards (Luke 2:20).

Invite people to come up with some words that go with these two great surprises of discovering peace. Build up the words into a group poem by linking them to create compound adjectives that describe the people and the events in question. For example:

The starlight-dazed, sleep-deprived, angel-shocked shepherds
Hear of peace from the dark-dipped skies.
The curiosity-driven, singing-led, stable-surprised shepherds
See peace with their own eyes.

Other possible compound adjectives to work with might include hillside-resting, fear-paralysed, breath-stolen, angel-chorused, sheep-abandoning, lambs-bleating, promise-believing, message-echoing and so on.

Angel acrostics

The key points of the carol could be summarized in an acrostic poem. For example:

Angels suddenly appear
Not wanting them to fear
Glad tidings sing
Expect to find a baby king
Look in Bethlehem with us
Sing songs to baby Jesus

*

IDEAS FOR EXPLORING
THE CAROLS THROUGH DRAMA

AWAY IN A MANGER

Home and away

This short drama sketch is designed to help tease out the meaning behind the familiar words of the carol. You will need two actors, each holding a copy of the *Bethlehem Carol Sheet*.

Narrator: *(Pensively)* Away... a way... way, way away.
Absent... gone... not here... Oh, I don't get it!

Child: Hello!

Narrator: *(Startled)* Oh! Hello, there! Perhaps you can help me.

Child: I'll do my best...

Narrator: *(Opens the carol sheet at 'Away in a manger')* Well, it's this carol, you see. It starts 'Away in a manger'. I'm not sure what that means. Away—that's... 'not here', 'absent'. Absent in a manger—I don't get it.

Child: *(Reads carol sheet)* I think the manger was in Bethlehem.

Narrator: Bethlehem? Bethlehem? The carol doesn't mention Bethlehem.

Child: Mary and Joseph went to Bethlehem—that's where Jesus was born.

Narrator: Ah, well, there you are, then. The manger wasn't absent—it was present. It was Jesus who was away—away from home when he was born. *(Thinks)* Well, that's true—he was away from his heavenly home.

Child: *(Reads carol sheet)* Perhaps that's why the stars looked down where he lay?

Narrator: No mention of Mary, though. Or Joseph.

Child: Mary laid Jesus on a bed of hay.

Narrator: Well, that would explain it, then—mangers, hay, must have been a stable. No mention of that, either.

Child: *(Reads carol sheet)* There were cattle.

Narrator: Yes, well—that's definitely not in the Bible! Lowing cattle. Not exactly hygienic surroundings for a newborn baby, is it? Giving birth in a cattle stall! Whatever next?

Child: *(Reads carol sheet)* The baby awakes.

Narrator: Well, I'm not surprised! All that mooing going on—it's enough to waken any baby.

Child: But the little Lord Jesus, no crying he makes.

Narrator: Who says so? Most babies cry. Crying is what babies do—it's what they're best at. I don't think I've ever met a baby that didn't cry.

Child: Was Jesus a real baby?

Narrator: Of course he was! As real as you and me. But he was also God. *(Thinks)* Perhaps that's why the carol says he didn't cry. It's to make us think he was perfect—which, of course, he was, being God. But babies don't cry because they're naughty—they cry because they don't have any

 Reproduced with permission from *Bethlehem Carols Unpacked* published by BRF 2008 (978 1 84101 534 7) www.barnabasinchurches.org.uk

other way to tell us what they want.

Child: *(Reads carol sheet)* Hmmm… one moment Jesus is asleep on a bed of hay and the next he's looking down from the sky. What's all that about?

Narrator: You know what? I think you really *have* helped me to see why the 'away in a manger' bit is there! When Jesus grew up, he did amazing things and people began to realize that God was living among them. So, when Jesus died on the cross they were devastated. *(Pause)* But then he rose from the dead and went home to be with his heavenly Father.

Child: *(Reads carol sheet)* Is that why the carol turns into a prayer: 'Be near me, Lord Jesus, I ask thee to stay close by me for ever and love me, I pray'?

Narrator: Absolutely! Jesus is with us every day of our lives, looking after us and blessing us with his love.

Child: *(Reads carol sheet)* And he fits us for heaven to live with him there!

Narrator: Yes! As well as being with us every day of our lives, Jesus has prepared a place for us to be with him in heaven.

Child: Home and away.

Narrator: Precisely! *(They do a high five)*

GOD REST YOU MERRY, GENTLEMEN

Pass the message on

You could explore the idea of messengers passing the message on through a dramatic acrostic. For example, an acrostic for angels might be:

> *Auras of light*
> *News-bearing beings*
> *Guardian friends*
> *Eloquent singers*
> *Lyrical messengers*
> *Servants of God*

An acrostic for Isaiah might be:

> *In darkness we walked*
> *Shadows give way to light*
> *A child is born*
> *Injustice put right*
> *All-powerful Lord*
> *Heaven's chosen king*

Pass the message on by giving one line each to six pairs of volunteers and, later in the service, invite one person from each pair to speak out their line in order, thus recreating the acrostic. As the lines are spoken, the other person from each pair stands at the front and expresses that line though movement. Each movement is 'frozen' after it is completed. For example:

- Auras of light: *Shield eyes*
- News-bearing beings: *Hold hands in front with palms up in the shape of an open book*

- Guardian friends: *Hold arms out as if protecting*
- Eloquent singers: *Move hand outwards from throat*
- Lyrical messengers: *Stand with arms open wide*
- Servants of God: *Kneel*

- In darkness we walked: *Hold hands in front of eyes*
- Shadows give way to light: *Shield eyes*
- A child is born: *Pretend to cradle a baby*
- Injustice put right: *Stand straight with one hand held high*
- All-powerful Lord: *Raise both arms*
- Heaven's chosen king: *Kneel*

The message will then be told visually in the freeze-frame, as well as audibly through the words spoken out.

Who's been sleeping in my manger?

The Christmas pantomime first became popular during Victorian times. The pantomime originated from the comic dances of the Italian Commedia dell' Arte of the 16th to 18th centuries, and included such characters as Harlequin, Columbine, Scaramouche and Pierrot. It probably came to England from France, where it formed a burlesque as light relief within a serious play. It softened into freestanding acted fairytales during Victorian times and has become part of our modern Christmas culture.

Although it would not be appropriate to incorporate a Christmas pantomime into a carol service, a light-hearted, pantomime-style sketch such as the on the following pages requires only a short script and a few actors and provides a thought-provoking visual element to the service.

Cast

Three performers are needed: Daddy Ox (male), Mummy Ox (female) and Baby Ox (male or female).

Staging: props, costumes and effects

Kit the actors out with brown T-shirts and a few bits and bobs such as horns, udders or a tail to give an overall impression. The only props you need are three blankets.

Scene

A cattle shed in Bethlehem (with an overbooked inn next door), home to three oxen: Daddy Ox, Mummy Ox and Baby Ox. Mummy Ox and Baby Ox are seated on stage. Daddy Ox enters. He is cross.

Daddy: That's it. I've had it up to here. I can't take any more. Call the family to order!

Mummy: *(Jumps up, shouts)* All oxen fall in! *(Pause, clears throat)* On the double!

Baby: *(Gets up)* Oh, very well. *(Comes over and lines up next to Mummy Ox)*

Mummy: Oxen standing by. *(Salutes)*

Daddy: Well done, Mummy Ox.

Mummy: Thanks, Daddy Ox.

Daddy:: We all know what day it is tomorrow? *(Beat)* Baby Ox?

Baby: Census day.

Mummy: Ooh! I'm so excited—

Daddy: Quiet! I'm sorry to say I'm not excited. In fact, I'm fed up to the back teeth. Everyone's gone mad! Decorations, cards, presents. Lunacy!

Mummy: But census time is special. Everyone gathered together, distant relations you haven't seen for ages…

Daddy: Huh! Stuck indoors all day with your mad cow of an auntie? We'll all get stuffed with food, play some games till we all get bored. Then the arguments start. Not this year. We're going away.

Mummy: We can't go away on census day!

Baby: Where's your census spirit?

Daddy: It wore out when they started the countdown. 'Only 106 shopping days to go!' Not for us. There will be no census day. Grab your blankets—we're going out into the fields to get away from it all.

Mummy Ox and Baby Ox go to fetch their blankets.

Mummy: Sorry, love. But you know what he's like.

Baby: Yes. I do think he's right in some ways. But I have a strange feeling that if we go away we might miss out on something special…

Mummy: I think his mind's made up.

They grab their blankets and move over to Daddy Ox.

Daddy: Let's go somewhere on earth where we can get some peace. Goodbye, lowly cattle shed. Shut the door on the way out, please, Ox junior.

They exit. Baby Ox shuts the door. Time passes. They return, a few days later. Mummy and Daddy enter with blankets wrapped around themselves. Baby has no blanket.

Daddy: I thought I told you to shut the door! Were you born in a barn?

Baby: I'm an ox, so of course I was!

Daddy: *(To Mummy)* How rude! Did you hear that?

Mummy: Well, you haven't given us a moment's peace since we left!

Daddy: After all I've done to give you a stable home to live in, a stable environment to grow up in, a stable… *(thinks)* stable.

Baby: I'm freezing.

Daddy: That'll teach you to give your blanket away.

Baby: *(Looking around)* I'm sure I shut that door when I left.

Mummy: Some holiday. Tempest, storm and wind! I feel like I haven't slept in a week.

Daddy: What were those shepherds shouting at by night?

Mummy: I don't know. I hid under my blanket after the light show began.

Daddy: Then they started the karaoke! What were those strange visitors singing? I'll give them 'peace on earth'! How about goodwill to oxen who are trying to get a good night's kip? Not exactly the restful break I hoped it would be.

Baby: Someone's been in here!

Mummy: It wasn't that bad. We did meet that nice little donkey on the dusty road.

Daddy: Sounded like he was having a worse census time than us. Carrying that young woman and her unborn baby for miles to Bethlehem. They hadn't even made a booking! There'll be no room at the inn, I said… not on census day!

Baby: Come over here and look! *(Points at straw)*

 Reproduced with permission from *Bethlehem Carols Unpacked* published by BRF 2008 (978 1 84101 534 7)
www.barnabasinchurches.org.uk

Daddy: Hang on! Someone's been sleeping in my straw!

Mummy: *(Comes over)* And someone's been sleeping in my straw!

Baby: *(Comes over)* And someone's been sleeping in my manger!

Daddy: And they're still there! *(Beat)* No, hang on a sec—it's just a blanket. *(Examines blanket)*

Baby: That's my blanket!

Daddy: I thought you gave it to the donkey—for when the baby was born?

Baby: They must have stayed here. The young couple with the donkey, they must have had their baby here!

Daddy: Yes… those strange people who sang to the shepherds, they said something about a baby. But they said he was a king.

Mummy: A king! Born here? Not in this poor lowly stable!

Baby: Hmm. Daddy Ox, you were so anxious to get away from all the festivities that we've missed out on a wonderful thing. A new king was born. And we could have welcomed him in, joined the celebrations. Now we've missed it all!

'WHO'S BEEN SLEEPING IN MY MANGER?' FROM *ALL-AGE SKETCHES FOR THE CHRISTIAN YEAR* BY PETER SHAW (BARNABAS, 2006).

GOOD KING WENCESLAS

Action mime

The carol is already in dramatic form and, to reflect this, is often sung with a bass for the words of the king and a treble or soprano to sing the page's lines. Everyone else sings the other verses. Clearly the carol then lends itself to being acted out with three main characters 'on stage' while everyone else sings the chorus and the parts. The three mime actors are the poor man picking up sticks, the king and his page.

To add to the visual effect, perhaps a white sheet could be put on the ground to give the impression of snow—deep and crisp and even. A single light could be shone down from a high spot to represent the brightly shining moon, and some Christmas goodies need to be available for the page to collect and carry when he is asked to do so by the king. Some dark footstep outlines could be discreetly scattered behind the king as he walks with the page to make visual 'his master's steps' and, finally, some sound effects of the wind blowing could be included (the wind is mentioned unfavourably twice in the carol). All this, with a few simple actions from the characters on stage, which would need minimal rehearsal (such as the king looking out, the page pointing to the poor man's home 'a good league hence' and some determined deep snow walking), would add a powerful dimension to the singing of the carol.

Read all about it!

On the surface, the Wenceslas carol presents us with a simple lesson about generosity to those in need. Its theme is picked up by many charities at this time of year, whose appeals urge us not to forget others in our headlong rush to spend, spend, spend on 'the best Christmas ever'. In Acts 20:35, the apostle Paul reminds his audience at Miletus of Jesus' teaching, namely, 'More blessings come from giving than from receiving.' Christmas can remind us of the pleasure of giving to others as opposed simply to receiving. However, giving isn't that easy and the carol draws this out in several ways.

Some of the challenges to giving are captured in the following short sketch, as King Wenceslas is interviewed about his Boxing Day kindness.

Cast

King Wenceslas, an interviewer, and three newspaper headline readers from the *Czech Gazette* (A, B and C), who open and close the sketch by calling out the news.

A:　　　　Coldest winter for 40 years!

B:　　　　Czech Rail reports the wrong kind of snow!

C:　　　　Prague Palace cut off by snowdrifts!

A:　　　　Latest weather reports: lunch, dinner and breakfast with frost!

B:　　　　Christmas misery for commuters!

C:　　　　Central Europe caught in big freeze!

Interviewer: Tell us, King Wenceslas, how did your St Stephen's Day charity begin?

Wenceslas: Well, it was because I was on the lookout.

Interviewer: What exactly did you see?

Wenceslas: I saw a man who was struggling to survive. He was looking for bits of wood to make a fire. He really needed help,

Interviewer: So, what exactly did you do?

Wenceslas: I asked around. I found out what this man's situation was—where he lived, what he needed. I couldn't just ignore what I'd seen.

Interviewer: What was your plan?

Wenceslas: Well, I had so much. Here in the west of the kingdom, we have more than enough, far more than we need. So I ordered the biggest food parcel ever to be put together...

Interviewer: How could you be sure that what you were doing would help?

Reproduced with permission from *Bethlehem Carols Unpacked* published by BRF 2008 (978 1 84101 534 7)
www.barnabasinchurches.org.uk
149

Wenceslas: There was only one thing for it: I had to go myself. I had to take the food there personally. Anyway, I don't believe in 'hands-free' giving.

Interviewer: You mean you went all the way yourself?

Wenceslas: Yes... with my page. I couldn't stand idly by and do nothing. This man was in need and I had something I could give. I had to take steps to help... big steps... deep steps...

Interviewer: And that was it? I mean... just *one* man helped? But there are so many people in need out there. Did this really make any difference?

Wenceslas: It made a difference to him. That's all I can say.

A: Wenceslas: Picnic King at Christmas!

B: King orders pizzas all round—deep and crisp and even!

C: King leaves prints to follow!

HARK! THE HERALD-ANGELS SING

Living in darkness

Use this series of short sketches scattered throughout the service. They should be very slapstick. The two characters can't see a thing because it's so dark. During the talk, you could pick up on the following themes:

- The pain of 'living in darkness'.
- What light (or inspiration or vision or insight) have you experienced?
- If you have experienced the light in some way, have you allowed it to change your life?
- How much are you influenced by others' cynicism?

Those living in darkness...

1 and 2 enter, tripping up.

1: Ouch!
2: Ow!
1: Where am I?
2: Who cares?
1: What time is it?
2: Dunno. Who cares?
1: I can't see a thing!
2: That's life, kiddo.
1: I can't even see you. Where are you?

1 flails arms about trying to find 2, and hits 2 by mistake.

2: Ouch! *(Hits 1 back on purpose)*
1: Ow!

They both exit, moaning.

... in the valley of the shadow...

1 and 2 enter from opposite sides and crash into each other.

1: Ouch!
2: Ow!
1: I'm fed up. First you thump me round the ear.
2: Sorry...
1: Then I fall down that hole...
2: And you trip over the dog.
1: Then I crash into a lamp-post...

2: And you go into the gents'/ladies by mistake.

1: What am I doing wrong?

2: This is life! This is as good as it gets!

1: It's got to be easier than this. Here, give me your hand…

2: Ouch! *(as 1 hits 2 again by mistake)*

1: Ow! *(as 2 hits 1 back)*

They both exit, moaning.

… have seen a great light

1 and 2 enter, groping along in the darkness, and accidentally squeeze each other's nose.

1: Ouch!

2: Ow!

1: Right, that's it. I've had enough.

2: So? It's going to be like this for ever and ever. Always dark…

1: There must be something we can do… some way out… *(1 searches in the darkness)*

2: Doomed to darkness for eternity. Doom… doom!

1: No! Look!

2: Doom… doom… Where?

1: There! *(1 points and knocks 2 on the head)*

2: Ouch! *(2 hits 1 back)*

1: Ow! What was that for? Ow!

They both exit, moaning.

 Reproduced with permission from *Bethlehem Carols Unpacked* published by BRF 2008 (978 1 84101 534 7)
www.barnabasinchurches.org.uk

Losing the vision

1 and 2 enter and bump into each other.

1: Ouch!

2: Ow!

1: Not again! How many years have we been hurting each other?

2: Too many!

1: Do you remember, all that time ago, you said you saw something?

2: When?

1: Oh! Years ago! Round about Christmas time, wasn't it?

2: I never found out what it was.

1: No.

2: Well?

1: You'll only laugh at me.

2: Go on! What was it?

1: I thought I saw a light…

2: A light?

1: It was a huge light! A massive light! Really bright! Just waiting for me! It would have changed everything!

2: A great light?

1: Yeah. It was… great!

2: Superstitious rubbish.

1: Oh. Yeah.

2: Too much Christmas sherry, eh?

1: Yeah.

2: Seasonal goodwill sending you a bit sentimental?

1: I expect so.

2: Light!

1: Ha ha.

2: A great light!

1: Ha ha.

2: You daft thing! (*2 swipes 1 on the back*)

1: Ouch! (*1 hits 2 back*)

2: Ow!

They both exit, moaning.

O COME, ALL YE FAITHFUL

O come!

This whole carol is an urgent invitation for us to join in the excitement of Christmas. The words 'O come' will have been sung no fewer than 16 times by the end of the carol. The following short sketch picks up the excitement of Christmas, particularly within the context of many people's reluctance to take up the invitation.

You will need five people for the sketch. One of these is the urgent inviter and the other four the reluctant invitees. It works well if the inviter moves around the worship space inviting everyone to come, and then the different invitees stand up and speak from within the congregation.

Inviter: (*Singing some of the first verse of the carol*)
'O come, all ye faithful,
Joyful and triumphant;
O come ye, O come ye to Bethlehem…' Are you coming? What about you? Do come! Come on! Come and join us.

Invitee A: Come? Come off it! I'm not coming anywhere. I'm far too busy. Don't you realize it's Christmas?

There's just so much to do. The cards to write, the cake to bake, the presents to wrap, the food to buy, the house to decorate…

Inviter: But do come! Come! Christmas is about more than all this. *(Continues to sing the first verse)* 'Come and behold him, born the king of angels…' Are you coming? What about you? Do come! Come on! Come and join us.

Invitee B: Come? Come off it! I'm not coming anywhere. In fact, I'm *going*! It's just too much to cope with. So I'm off. Christmas in the Bahamas for me, not Bethlehem! It's a crazy time of year. I'm not getting sucked into it again. I'm swapping the Queen's Speech for a Caribbean beach! Give me bright sunlight and peace and paradise!

Inviter: But do come! Come! Christmas is so special. It's all those things you want. It's about a very bright light and peace and paradise. Light from light… heaven on earth… Are you coming? What about you? Do come! Come on! Come and join us.

Invitee C: Come? Come off it! I don't need all this. I'm going to have a great time anyway, thanks very much. I don't need all this theology getting in the way! It's a party time of year. Music and dancing, drinking and clubbing. No time for this carol-singing nonsense!

Inviter: But do come! Come! Christmas is the biggest party ever. Everyone's involved. All of heaven will be there. It's the party to end all parties. Are you coming? What about you? Do come! Come on! Come and join us.

Invitee D: Come? Come off it. You can't mean me. I don't get invitations any more. Why should anyone invite me? Besides, I'm happy with my TV and radio at home. I'll just shut up shop behind closed doors till it's all over—like last year.

Inviter: But do come! Come. It *is* for you! It's for all of us. This is God's party. God has come to be with us! Everyone matters to God! Christmas tells us this. You, me, shepherds, babies, angels... everybody! Come on! Come! Don't miss out on the greatest invitation ever. (*Sings again*) 'Come ye, O come ye to Bethlehem; come and behold him, born the King of angels.'

Inviter encourages everyone to join in the singing of the final chorus:

All: O come, let us adore him,
O come, let us adore him,
O come, let us adore him,
Christ the Lord!'

O LITTLE TOWN OF BETHLEHEM

Stars and angels

This carol includes both silent and singing stars ('O morning stars, together proclaim the holy birth'). It also includes angels keeping watch and angels telling glad tidings. The following simple drama can involve children and adults together, becoming those very stars and angels from the story, moving us from peaceful reverence to song-filled proclamation.

 Reproduced with permission from *Bethlehem Carols Unpacked* published by BRF 2008 (978 1 84101 534 7) www.barnabasinchurches.org.uk

You can have as many people being angels and stars as can move comfortably about your worship space. The stars should gather on the left, moving eventually towards the front, where they should stand elevated in some way, perhaps on a bench. The angels should move similarly from the right, eventually gathering in front of the stars. The stars should carry star shapes made from six bamboo sticks entwined with tinsel and tied together to create a six-pointed star. The angels should be in white T-shirts and trousers.

Finally, there is a narrator whose words should be spoken over a microphone, but who should remain out of sight. For the first part of the drama, the music of the carol should be playing quietly in the background. When the stars and angels eventually sing, they will sing to the music of the carol, but with some new words.

Narrator: *(In a hushed, reverential tone)* Shh! Shh! Something amazing is about to happen. Bethlehem is the chosen place. It is the dead of night. The night sky is full of stars.

Stars gather on the left, whispering to each other and looking about. Their words should be spoken by a variety of different voices from among the group.

Stars: Shh! Shh! Bethlehem's the place. Bethlehem's the place. Don't wake anyone. Quietly now. Bethlehem's the place.

Stars move about quietly on the left of the worship space.

Narrator: *(Hushed reverential voice)* Shh! Shh! Something amazing has happened. A baby has been born. The everlasting light is shining, and the angels are keeping watch.

Angels gather to the right of the worship space, whispering to each other. Their words should be spoken by a variety of different voices from among the group.

Angels: Shh! Shh! The baby is born. The everlasting light is a baby! Wow! Look! How amazing! Shh! Don't disturb them yet.

Angels tiptoe about, pointing in amazement at something below them, as they move on the right of the worship space.

Narrator: *(Slightly louder and with urgency)* Listen, listen! Something incredible is happening. It's just like at the beginning. The stars are singing again!

The stars should move forward from the left of the worship space to take their position at the front on a bench. As they do this, they should sing the following new words to the melody of this carol.

Stars: We first sang out so long ago
When God made all we see,
And now it's time to welcome here
The gift of this baby.
Our God is making all things new,
Creation starts again.
A light is shining in their hearts
To take away all blame.

Narrator: *(Even more urgently)* Listen, listen! Something totally unheard of is happening. We can hear angels singing on earth. Heaven can keep silent no longer.

Angels move from the right of the worship space to take up their position in front of the stars. As they move, they sing the following new words to the melody of the carol.

Angels: Peace on earth, good news for all,
Jesus, the Christ, has come.
This birth will give a brand new start
On earth for everyone.
Let all the world hear this good news
That Jesus Christ is here.
God is with them, as God's with us
For all both far and near.

Narrator: *(In total amazement)* Even the stars sang when Jesus was born! And the angels sang when Jesus was born! There were Christmas carols in space and time!

All   O morning stars, together proclaim the holy birth.
We hear the Christmas angels the great glad tidings tell.
O come to us, abide with us, our Lord Emmanuel.

ONCE IN ROYAL DAVID'S CITY

To earth from heaven

Perform the following piece of drama with a narrator and a group of actors.

As the narrator suggests each image in the first section, the group of actors take up a pose. For example, for an elephant, one might swing their arms for a trunk, with four others making the legs and two people holding their arms curved to make huge ears. You might like to swap items for shapes that your team particularly enjoys making.

Narrator: Imagine the biggest thing in the world... an elephant... the Eiffel Tower... no, a blue whale... the Grand Canyon... a volcano... a deep sea rift in the ocean floor... a space rocket... a doubledecker bus... a tyrannosaurus rex...

In the next section, the acting team work together to show the different dimensions. For example, for 'wide', they might hold hands and spread out in a line reaching out to the sides as far as they can. For the last sentence about being dressed in baby clothes, the acting team form a traditional nativity tableau, Mary miming the part of holding a very small Jesus.

Narrator: Now imagine something that high, that deep, that wide, that powerful, that beautiful, that terrifying, that unstoppable, that magnificent, that amazing, that BIG... dressed in baby clothes and held in a young girl's arms.

SILENT NIGHT

Silent night?

You will need to cast the narrator, Joseph, Mary, and shepherds. You will also need sound effects, which could either be provided by 'live' voices or be recorded in advance. The sound effects are rustling straw, an ox, a donkey, a cockerel, some sheep and the cry of a baby.

 Reproduced with permission from *Bethlehem Carols Unpacked* published by BRF 2008 (978 1 84101 534 7) www.barnabasinchurches.org.uk

The melody of 'Silent night' plays as Mary and Joseph take their places in a traditional nativity crib scene.

Narrator: Here we are, with the little town of Bethlehem lying still around us in a deep and dreamless sleep. The silent stars are going by. Snow has fallen, snow on snow, thus muffling any sounds that might otherwise have been heard, and making it look terribly scenic, too. Yon Virgin Mother is sitting gracefully on a small clean stool. The holy infant has been born and is sleeping in heavenly peace. All is calm; all is bright.

Joseph: Shh!

Narrator: I'm the narrator! I have to narrate!

Joseph: It's only just gone quiet!

Narrator: I know! The baby is sleeping in heavenly peace. I'm telling everyone what a silent night it is.

Joseph: Silent? Here? Are you mad?

Narrator: 'How silently, how silently the wondrous gift is given…'

Joseph: Apart from the odd shriek of a birthing mother and servants clattering in with hot water and towels… and half the guests at the inn deciding to have a drinking party in the street outside. Oh, and the innkeeper barging in, banging the door, checking we weren't stealing his oxen. And the Roman soldiers changing guard every few hours… yes, it's been very silent.

Sound effects of rustling in the straw.

Reproduced with permission from *Bethlehem Carols Unpacked* published by BRF 2008 (978 1 84101 534 7)
www.barnabasinchurches.org.uk

Narrator: What was that rustle?
Joseph: Rats. It's a stable. There are rats.
Narrator: Rats??

Sound effects of mooing.

Joseph: Oh, you've woken the ox, and it took me hours
              to shut it up.
Narrator: But it's supposed to be a silent night!
Joseph: Will you just…?

Sound effects of the hee-haw of a donkey. The ox continues to moo.

Joseph: There! Now it's the donkey, too. Have you got a
              carrot? It's the only way to quieten it down. As
              I was saying…
Narrator: No, as *I* was saying…

Sound effects of a cockerel crowing to add to donkey and ox.

Joseph: Shh! Quiet! Now the cockerel thinks it's
              morning! *(To the cockerel)* Is it morning? I don't
              think so! So why are you crowing? *(To the
              narrator)* Look…

Sound effects of sheep baaing as well as the cockerel, donkey and ox.

Joseph: Sheep? Where did *they* come from?
Shepherds: *(Banging on the door)* Hello? Can we come in?
              We're looking for the Saviour.
Joseph: What?

 Reproduced with permission from *Bethlehem Carols Unpacked* published by BRF 2008 (978 1 84101 534 7)
www.barnabasinchurches.org.uk

Shepherds: The Saviour! The angels said to go and find the Saviour...

Joseph: But...!

Narrator: Ah! Shepherds first saw the sight!

Shepherds: There he is! Eh, what a bonny lad. *(They chat away happily)*

Joseph: Shh! We don't want him to wake up and start crying again.

Narrator: It's Jesus! 'The little Lord Jesus, no crying he makes.'

Joseph: He's a baby! Babies cry! It's what they do best! And take it from me—our Jesus is already very good at it!

Narrator: You're spoiling my nice narration!

All this time, the moos, heehaws, crows, baas and shepherds are getting louder so that Joseph has to shout over the top.

Joseph: Oh, for heaven's sake... get real. This isn't about nice. It's not about silence. Or peace. If God wanted peace, he'd have kept his Son in heaven. Not sent him down here into the bustle and hubbub and NOISE...

The baby cries. Other noises die away in shock, as Mary lifts up the baby, who goes quiet.

Mary: Hush, Jesus, hush. There... there... time enough for noise later on in your life, son. Time enough for shouts and cheers from the crowds. Time for stormy seas and angry mobs, for the clash of steel and the hammering of nails. There will be a time for all these things. But praise God, it's not now. For now, for this one brief moment, let's treasure the transforming peace your birth has brought us.

THE FIRST NOWELL

Revealing the cross

Here is an idea for creating mime actions for the carol. If you have a nativity crib scene, this will form the centrepiece for the action. If not, choose a centre point at the front as the nativity area. You will need to choose some angels, some shepherds and three wise men to perform the mime. You will also need a large star for the angels to hold, on the reverse side of which the outline of a cross has been drawn.

First of all, in verse 1, the angels sing the chorus. As they are singing, they move towards some people (the shepherds) who are 'asleep' on the back pews and then lead them up to the nativity scene.

During the singing of verse 2, the angels hold up a large star shape, move towards people in the church porch or doorway and lead them to the centre. They sing the chorus as they come to the front.

In verse 3, the people from the porch or doorway kneel and offer gifts and the angels sing the chorus.

Finally, in verse 4, with everyone singing, as many people as possible approach the nativity scene or centre point. The angels now turn the star they are holding to reveal the outline of a cross on the reverse side.

 Reproduced with permission from *Bethlehem Carols Unpacked* published by BRF 2008 (978 1 84101 534 7) www.barnabasinchurches.org.uk

WE THREE KINGS

Star maker

This idea for a Christmas presentation links the miracle of Christmas with the mystery of Easter. It tries to put the Christmas story into the context of the bigger picture of God coming down to earth as Jesus, not just to be born but also to die for us. The presentation will need rehearsal and involves at least six children or adults and one or more narrators.

You will need six plank-like pieces of wood or card (four shorter pieces and two longer pieces). When the children and adults hold these pieces together, they are going to create various patterns and shapes in a vertical plane, which must be large enough for the whole congregation to see. As a guide to size, the shorter pieces should be 1m by 20cm and the longer pieces should be 1.5m by 20cm. On one side the pieces should all be a dark brown colour and on the other side they should all be bright yellow or gold.

The shapes that will be made are two stars, a manger, a table, a cross, and a cross and star together. Here's how to form them with the six pieces. (This will need practice beforehand.)

For the first star

The children and adults should hold the pieces on a vertical plane so that they create a star with eight rays. Use the two longer pieces to create an equal-armed cross as the centre, pointing north, south, east and west like a compass. The other four pieces radiate out, north-east, north-west, south-east, south-west. For this star shape, it is the yellow or gold side that should face the congregation.

For the second star

As above, but this time it is the brown side that faces the congregation.

For the manger or crib

Again this shape is to be seen on a vertical plane, so use the two longer pieces for the top and bottom parts of the crib and the four other pieces for the two sides and two legs splaying outwards. To do this, some of the group will need to stand and some will need to kneel to enable the shape to be formed as they hold the pieces. For the crib or manger, it is the brown side of the pieces that faces the congregation.

For the table

The shape will be seen on a vertical plane in cross-section. Place the two longer pieces horizontally on top of each other to be the surface of the table, while the four smaller pieces become legs going downwards below. For the table, it is the brown side again that faces the congregation.

For the cross

Seen on a vertical plane: hold the two longer pieces together vertically, one above the other. Two-thirds of the way up, place two of the shorter pieces together horizontally on one side, and the other two on the other side. The brown side should be facing the congregation.

For the star and cross together

Recreate the star shape as before, but this time the two central, longer pieces in the cross shape should have their brown side facing the congregation, while the shorter pieces show their gold or yellow side.

Once the shapes are well rehearsed, they should be formed at each stage to accompany the following narration, which could be shared between two or more speakers:

First star   *(Yellow/gold)* The star maker smiled. It was just
                as he planned it. Swirling galaxies, beautiful
                suns, myriads of planets and endless space. All
                was light—bright, clean and pure. Each star
                named and numbered; each star reflecting his
                glory.

Second star   *(Brown)* But then the star maker watched as one
                star, with its solar system, dawned. His face
                saddened as he watched it come out. This star
                began to dim. Darkness was putting out the
                light. It no longer shone as he had planned.

Manger   *(Brown)* The star maker knew what he must do.
                He took off his own light and made himself
                very small. He sent himself down into the
                emptiness and became a thing that he had
                made. He shared the experience of being in the
                dark. The star maker chose to lie helpless on
                starlit hay, and the people of the darkness called
                it 'Christmas'.

Table   *(Brown)* The star maker grew up and tasted the
                dark life, shining back at it with his own inner
                light. He made tables in a carpenter's
                workshop. He sat around a family table in a
                poor home. He was invited to meals with
                people of all sorts. He shared the light of
                heaven and, at a table in an upper room, he
                talked about bread and wine.

Cross   (*Brown*) Finally he went into battle with the
               darkness. Taking on all that was bad, he even
               let his own light be put out. The star maker
               became the sin breaker, and he who made the
               stars became scarred to bring back the light.

Cross inside star (*Brown inside yellow/gold*) The star maker
               won the victory and, after the battle, the light
               began to shine again in this part of his creation.
               That light shines in the darkness still and the
               darkness has not overcome it, because
               Christmas is only the star-t.

WHILE SHEPHERDS WATCHED

Setting the scene

The carol can be used as a sung narrative to accompany the setting
up of your nativity scene. For example, verse 1 could be sung as the
shepherds gather and react to the angels in a part of the worship
space, to one side of the place where the nativity tableau will be
presented.

Verse 2 could be sung as the first angel takes up a high position
(perhaps in the pulpit or on top of some safe stepladders draped in
black cloth).

Verse 3 could be sung as the angel points to the place where the
nativity scene will be, within which a manger can now be placed
and assorted animal characters begin to gather.

Verse 4 could be sung as Mary and Joseph and the baby take up
their positions, laying the baby in the manger on cue with the last
line of this verse.

Verse 5 could be sung as more angels appear and gather around the nativity scene.

Finally, verse 6 could be sung as everyone joins in with the angels' chorus, with a fully assembled nativity cast.

*

IDEAS FOR EXPLORING THE CAROLS THROUGH CREATIVE WORSHIP

Held in Jesus' care

You will need: packs of card stars (available from office stationers), two or three bread baskets, pens or pencils, sticky tack and a large board covered with black sugar paper.

Place the stars in the baskets, making sure there are enough for everyone present. Invite everyone to take a star as they come into the worship space. Have the pens or pencils ready to distribute as needed. Place the board covered with black sugar paper at the front of the worship space and have the sticky tack nearby.

After the singing of the carol, ask everyone to write on the star the name of a person they want Jesus to hold in his care. Play the melody of the carol through gently and invite everyone to offer that person to Jesus' care by fixing the star to the black board. Finish with the following prayer.

Lord Jesus, thank you that you were prepared to leave your heavenly home to live among us. Thank you for everything you have taught us about God, your heavenly Father. We lift the people whose names are written on these stars to you today. Please stay close by them for ever and love them. Bless each person named with your love and care and fit each one of us for heaven, to live with you there. Amen

GOD REST YOU MERRY, GENTLEMEN

Seasonal senses

The themes of this carol can be threaded through the service using the five senses.

Touch

Carol services are typically attended by many visitors as well as the regular congregation. One way to start the service might be to invite the congregation to introduce themselves to those around them and to offer a hand in blessing, thus passing the peace to each other in an informal yet non-threatening way. Alternatively, you could invite everyone to share God's peace towards the end of the service with those sitting around them. This could be done before the final carol as a way to help people chat naturally to those who are visiting, once the service is over.

Taste

Serve foods associated with traditional Christmas fare after the service, such as mince pies, small slices of plum pudding or fruit cake, or small sweets such as sugar mice in Christmassy petit four cases.

Sight

Display pictures of an old-fashioned Christmas around the worship space and use them as a starting point to talk about Christmas traditions—how have things changed, what remains the same and so on. Point out that, however the celebration of Christmas has changed through the years, the message always remains the same.

Sound

Print out the words of Isaiah 9:6–7, breaking the passage into approximately six sentences (depending on which translation you use), with each sentence on a separate sheet of paper. The CEV is a good translation to use for this exercise.

Pass on the message around the congregation as follows: split the congregation into six blocks (or however many sentences there are in your chosen Bible version), with roughly the same number of people in each block. Give each block one sentence from the passage and ask them to pass it along from person to person, the first person saying it to their neighbour and so on until everyone has heard and passed on the message. Ask them to do this out loud and simultaneously so that the worship space buzzes with the sound of the message being passed on.

Smell

Invite people to suggest smells that remind them of Christmas, such as winter walks, Christmas foods, scented candles, wrapping paper, freshly picked evergreens and so on. Draw together the different suggestions with a prayer of thanksgiving for the smells that remind us of the good news of Jesus' birth.

GOOD KING WENCESLAS

In the tenth century, Wenceslas was a duke of Bohemia, which is the same geographical area as the Czech Republic today. Several features of a traditional Christmas in this part of the world could be used to encourage some thoughtful worship.

Open-handed day

The traditional names for Christmas Eve and Christmas Day in the Czech language translate as 'open-handed day' and 'God's feast day'. Worshippers could represent these two days by the way they hold their hands. For example:

- Hands held up to receive, representing the feast in which we share.
- Hands held out to give, representing the gifts we are called to share.

Using these gestures, encourage the congregation first to give thanks for the good things of Christmas (the feast day) and then to think of the people we should care for, who are in any kind of need at Christmas (the open-handed day). Encourage some ideas to be shared out loud. Collect all the suggestions together with the following words and with hands in the appropriate positions.

- For all the joy and good gifts of Christmas we praise you, O Lord.
- For those in need at Christmas, show us how to reveal your love, O Lord.

Christmas gifts

In many European countries, Father Christmas (Santa Claus) comes earlier in the month, on 5 or 6 December, which is when St Nicholas' day is celebrated (5 December in the Netherlands, and 6 December in Belgium and Germany). The idea of present-giving on 5 or 6 December dates from the legend of St Nicholas, a fourth-century bishop, who is supposed to have put money into the stockings of some poor girls whose father had no money for their dowries. This legend is the origin of the Christmas stocking. In Britain and some other countries, this custom has been combined with giving presents on Christmas Day. We can use these gifts to help to refocus the festival on the Bible story. The gifts become symbols of the great gift of Jesus to the world, or reminders that as the wise men gave gifts to Jesus, so we give presents to each other.

Wrap up several differently sized boxes in gift paper, and pile them by the Christmas tree. Invite children and adults to come and pick out a box from the pile and share ideas of what gifts they think the world needs from God today. (For example, peace, hope, understanding and friendship might be among the suggestions.) After these gifts from Jesus have been shared, draw the time of worship to a conclusion with the following words.

All these gifts were wrapped up for us in the name of Jesus at Christmas. Show us the way to unwrap these gifts for the world through lives of generosity and service in the year ahead. Amen

Apples

Another tradition in the Czech Republic is to cut apples in half crosswise as part of the celebrations and see what shape appears in each half. It might resemble a star or a cross. Invite a group from the congregation to come and do this and show everyone the results of their cutting. Use the activity as a way into the mystery of Christmas. There is both the star that declares the glory of God and the cross that reveals how that glory will save the world.

Picking out some key phrases from the Christmas story, members of the group should lift up a corresponding apple half with the symbol of cross or star, which matches a phrase, for example, 'glory to God' (star), 'born a Saviour' (cross), 'God Most High' (star), 'his name will be Jesus' (cross), 'good news, which will make everyone happy' (star), 'peace on earth' (cross), 'dayspring from on high' (star) and 'she gave birth to her firstborn' (cross).

HARK! THE HERALD-ANGELS SING

A liturgy of light

Put tealight candles into jam jars and place them around the worship space. As people come in, have a PowerPoint slideshow of light and dark images, such as a lighthouse, car headlights, a torch, a lantern, a candle, a laser display, a searchlight, an emergency exit sign, a star, the sun and moon, a smiling face, a street lamp, or the Narnian lamp-post.

As you open the service, turn off the lights so that you have a feel for the darkness. Play an appropriate piece of music, such as 'The people who walked in darkness have seen a great light' from Handel's *Messiah*, or a more modern song such as 'Light of the world, you stepped down into darkness' by Tim Hughes. As the music plays, carry in a lighted candle. Light the candles around the worship space and gradually bring up the houselights until the climax of the song is sung in a blaze of light. As the song finishes, readers from around the worship space could call out the Bible verses in the Bible links (see page 62).

Opening sentences

Leader: Let us shout with the herald-angels:
All: Glory to the newborn king!

Leader: Let us join with all the nations of earth and all the hosts of heaven
All: Glory to the newborn king!

Leader: Let us worship Jesus together, our Emmanuel, our God-with-us
All: Glory to the newborn king!

Leader: When we can choose light or darkness
All: We choose the light.

Leader: When we find ourselves in the shadows
All: We choose the light.

Leader: When our thoughts turn towards the darkness
All: We choose to turn them to the light.

Leader: When our actions can bring light or darkness to those around us
All: We choose to bring light.

Leader: When our words can bring light or darkness to those around us
All: We choose to bring light.

Leader: God of light and life, you set prisoners free from their dark dungeons to see the light of day. Shine your light in our thoughts and words and actions. Light up our imagination and our courage so that we may shine like the noonday sun for you and for those around us.

Reading from *Some Other Rainbow*

I was to be in this solitary cell for less than three months, but after the first two or three weeks it felt as if I had slipped into a different time-scale. Days passed without any variation. The food-and-bathroom run and then nothing. I read and re-read everything available. I relived much of my life and made endless plans for the future. But after two months with not the slightest hint that I might be released I got more frightened. So many of my reflections had left me feeling inadequate that I began to doubt that I could cope alone.

One morning these fears became unbearable. I stood in the cell sinking into despair. I felt that I was literally sinking, being sucked down into a whirlpool. I was on my knees, gasping for air, drowning in hopelessness and helplessness. I thought that I was passing out. I could only think of one thing to say—'Help me please, oh God, help me.' The next instant I was standing up, surrounded by a warm bright light. I was dancing, full of joy. In the space of a minute, despair had vanished, replaced by boundless optimism.

What had happened? I had never had any great faith, despite a Church of England upbringing. But I felt that I had to give thanks. But to what? Unsure of the nature of the experience, I felt most comfortable acknowledging the Good Spirit which seemed to have rescued me.

It gave me great strength to carry on and, more importantly, a huge renewal of hope—I was going to survive. Throughout my captivity, I would take comfort from this experience, drawing on it whenever optimism and determination flagged. In the euphoria of the next few days I felt completely confident. But soon I found myself wondering how, even with the support of a Good Spirit, I was going to manage alone.

FROM *SOME OTHER RAINBOW* BY JOHN MCCARTHY AND JILL MORRELL (BANTAM, 1993)

O COME, ALL YE FAITHFUL

Come to Bethlehem!

As a great invitation, this carol lends itself to some simple drama, which involves different groups coming to 'Bethlehem' from separate parts of the worship space. You could have mixed groups of children and adults ready for each verse, gathered in different corners of the worship space and then processing slowly to a central nativity scene, one group from the back and the others from the sides. You will need to map out the routes that each take, so that those representing verse 3 have less distance to travel than those representing verses 1 and 2.

Each group should be headed up by some children and adults who will be 'in character' for the central nativity tableaux, which they gradually build as they arrive.

For example: shepherds could lead the first group, Mary, Joseph and the baby could lead the second group and angels could lead group three. This will need some rehearsal, particularly with regard to the pace at which each processional group walks, but it will make a memorable start to your carol service.

You could take this activity one stage further by giving particular props to each of the groups, appropriate to the verses that they are singing. For example, in verse 1 celebration is the keynote, so the groups could be holding balloons and banners and have flags to wave Verse 2 is full of solemnity and symbol, so this group could carry candles and lanterns. Music is the keynote in verse 3, so this group could have musical instruments. Everyone should gather at the front around the nativity scene and join together for the last verse.

O LITTLE TOWN OF BETHLEHEM

The heart of Bethlehem

The four different focus points of the carol's four verses are:

- Bethlehem
- The baby
- Our hearts
- Our response

Such a reflective carol calls for some simple mime by a group of children or children and adults together. Each suggested mime below accompanies one verse of the carol.

- **Verse 1:** To create an image of Bethlehem, the group should stand as a perfect square, holding hands and with their heads leaning to one side, as if asleep.
- **Verse 2:** To portray the arrival of the child, a small group should creep along in a circle around one person holding an imaginary baby. They will need to bend low as they go underneath the arms of one side of the square that is Bethlehem. They should then kneel in a circle with the baby held in the middle, at the centre of the square.
- **Verse 3:** The square now reshapes itself into a large heart. To make this idea more visible, each member of the shape should hold both hands to their heart.
- **Verse 4:** The group in the centre with the baby should now stand and walk quietly up to the side of the heart shape, offering the baby to each person in turn during the singing of this verse.

ONCE IN ROYAL DAVID'S CITY

Choices

Set up tables with some or all of the following:

- **Touch:** a variety of rich fabrics and rough fabrics and textures. How do they feel on your skin? Which would you rather wear?
- **Taste:** a variety of luxury foods such as individual chocolates, small fruits, nuts, crisps, smoked salmon or ham, and some plain foods such as rough bread, rice, porridge or mashed potato. Taste the different foods. Which foods would make you happier?
- **Sight:** pictures of palaces and pictures of slums. Where would you most like to live?
- **Sound:** a CD of raucous traffic noise and one of gentle music. Which sound would you prefer to wake up to?
- **Smell:** Glossy pictures of rich perfumes and pictures of rotting rubbish. Which would you rather smell in your home?

Invite everyone to go to each table and spend some time making choices. Come back together and talk about what people chose. How hard would it be to leave the riches behind and deliberately choose poverty? You might include a short story about a Christian (for example, someone in your own congregation, a mission link, or someone famous such as St Francis of Assisi or Jackie Pullinger) who gave up riches in order to follow Christ.

These people followed God's own example: Jesus came down to earth from heaven to live with those in need. Draw your thoughts together with a read or sung version of the second verse of 'Once in royal David's city'.

Words and pictures

Find a selection of images of children in different situations of poverty, such as refugees, streetchildren, child soldiers, pregnant teenagers, orphans, children in droughtstricken areas, gangs and so on. Devise a slideshow of the images, using phrases from the carol, such as:

- His children
- He came down
- With the poor and mean and lowly
- Little, weak and helpless
- Like us
- Tears and smiles
- Dear and gentle
- He leads his children on
- Like stars his children crowned

It can be very powerful for the images to work against the words.

SILENT NIGHT

Heavenly peace

The peacefulness of this carol invites us to offer some peaceful worship to God and to enter his peace with him and with each other.

Either set up a nativity scene in a space of your building or, better still, have some silent actors dressed in unobtrusive costumes (not dressing gowns—either use realistic peasant-type, Middle Eastern clothes or ordinary, fairly timeless clothes).

As music plays behind your words, set the scene for everyone with the following story.

A baby was born in occupied territory, in desperate circumstances. His parents were driven far from home by the political demands of an unjust dictator. The baby was born into appalling poverty, far from professional medical help. It was an overcrowded house in a backstreet of a remote town. It was cold. It was filthy. It was a bad beginning.

But in those appalling circumstances, the baby was still surrounded and enfolded by loving care, as his mother dressed him in what few clothes she had and laid him in the warmest bed she could find.

That baby was born two thousand years ago, but the story goes on today in the mysterious way that true stories do. The baby is still being born. The circumstances for many of us are still hopeless and appalling, but love still surrounds us and enfolds us. And we can still enter this story. We can enter his peace and bring the troubles that we have into his peace to be transformed by it.

As the music plays, I invite you to come to this scene from the story and bring something of yourself to place in the peace of Jesus' presence. It might be something from your pocket or handbag, representing something only you and God know about. It might be a word or name that you write on a scrap of paper. It might be a glove or a hat that is simply something personal to you. But please bring something that you would like to leave in the peaceful presence of God. You can have it back at the end of the service, of course!

Dim the lights, if possible. Ceremoniously place a lantern or candle into the nativity scene. Play the melody of 'Silent night' as people bring their offerings, then sing the first verse quietly together when everyone has finished.

THE FIRST NOWELL

Gift boxes

For the offertory, have small collecting boxes at the end of each row, shaped like the items in which the wise men would have carried their gifts—a small box like a treasure chest, a perfume jar and a small bag. Collections can be made into these containers and brought up to the front.

Outsiders

Show pictures of outsiders alongside the singing of the carol. Look especially for pictures of orphans and refugees. (For downloadable images and more information about the work of Bible*Lands*, go to www.biblelands.org.uk.)

Pause for thought

Have a selection of sound effects to use as an introduction to the theme of the carol. They can be used reflectively before the carol is sung. For example:

- Sheep sounds, snoring, running and then gasping in amazement.
- Camels snorting, hooves trudging, saddles jangling, gasping in amazement.
- Flies buzzing, Egyptian street sounds, people talking, passports being stamped, sighs of relief and then gasping in amazement.

WE THREE KINGS

Sensory worship

Use some or all of these ideas to worship Jesus as represented in the three prophetic gifts given by the wise men: Jesus as king, God and sacrifice. Some of these activities have a slightly Orthodox slant, which, for many Christians in Western churches, may echo the 'otherness' of the wise men. We need to be prepared to appreciate ways of worship from all round the world.

Sight

There are many icons of Christ the King. Search for images on the Internet by inputting the words "Christ the king icon", and display one or a selection for reflection. You could include a simple question like 'What is this artist trying to show me about Jesus? What might Jesus be saying to me?'

Sound

Play some Christian music from another part of the world, such as Russian Orthodox chanting or African praise. Remember how alien the wise men were to Mary and Joseph, and yet they worshipped Jesus, too. Praise God that people from every nation can worship the same Jesus.

Smell

Incense has been used for thousands of years as a symbol of prayer— the smoke rising to God as our prayers rise to him. Many years before the birth of Jesus, the psalmist wrote, 'Think of my prayer as sweet-smelling incense' (Psalm 141:2). If you are unfamiliar with the use of incense in worship, find a local church that has a tradition of using it.

Ask if you can have some charcoal disks, a dish in which to burn them and a demonstration of how to get the incense to stay alight.

From the beginning of the service, have some incense brewing gently in a bowl, a good distance from the people. Invite everyone to watch the smoke rising and to wait for the fragrance to reach them. Remind them that worship is an experience that involves the whole body, not just the head and mouth.

Touch

Touch the skin of your own hand very deliberately and reflect on how God chose to come and fit into a human skin. What a sacrifice! What a God! What does that tell you about how much he is concerned when our bodies are not functioning properly? Ask God to comfort those who are unwell. Think about how we are tempted to misuse our bodies, especially at Christmas time, with too much to eat and drink.

Alternatively, if you prefer, buy some myrrh oil (available from some pharmacists) or ask your local pharmacist to suggest a suitable alternative. Invite people to rub the oil on to their hand. Ask them to feel the oiliness of it and to smell it.

Taste

Invite people to break off a piece of a rough loaf of bread and think about the way some Christians make a sacrifice of food when they fast. Ask people to pick up their piece of bread and then lay it down again. The bread reminds us of Jesus' sacrifice on the cross, through the bread he broke at the last supper.

They knelt down and worshipped him

Many people don't kneel in church these days. If kneeling to pray is not in your church's tradition, you might like to suggest that everyone tries it for one of the worship items in the service, perhaps a worship song or a prayer. Talk about why the wise men might have knelt and how it feels to kneel in worship.

Psalm 72

One of the wise men's gifts was gold, to symbolize kingship. Psalm 72 describes a great king. Read it through together and choose phrases from the psalm to worship Jesus the king.

WHILE SHEPHERDS WATCHED

Preparing for worship

What an array of sights, smells and sounds are wrapped up in this carol! From the earthy animal smells around the night fire to the dazzling splendour of angel choirs, there are plenty of sensory ways into the carol for congregations to explore, so that they can enter more fully into it as a piece of Christian worship.

To set the scene for this carol, it will be helpful to work through a series of simple sensory exercises first, as outlined below, before the congregation eventually sings it all through.

Start by encouraging a group of children and adults to sit down on the floor like the shepherds in the tale. Help them to feel the earth beneath them. Ask them to put on their outdoor clothes again or pull their jumpers and tops closely around them, as they imagine what it would feel like to be huddled together for warmth around the night-watch fire. Encourage the children to think about what was on the shepherds' minds that night.

The glow of flames suddenly begins to intensify and the flood-light glory of the angel messenger fills their horizon. This could be experienced in part by asking the congregation to focus for a while on a small candle flame at the front or in a position where all can see it clearly, and then to turn their eyes suddenly towards a large sheet of shiny silver paper on to which you have shone a strong and powerful light. What on earth did they think was happening? What terrors were going through their minds? What explanations for the phenomenon could they think of?

We don't know what an angel voice sounds like, but it probably wouldn't be tiny and feeble! You could prepare for this section of the carol by booming out the words of the angel messenger over the loudspeaker system in as mysterious and reverberating a style as the sound system or the human voice can manage. What a mixture of fear and wonder must have shaken the shepherds when they heard the angel's words! It was a sound they not only heard but also felt. What was the angel talking about? Why was the angel speaking to them? What had they got to do with the purposes of heaven?

Next comes the heavenly choir. There are a number of pieces of music you might choose for this. The appropriate extract from Handel's *Messiah* comes first to mind, but you might equally choose the 'Amen' that is part of *Spem in alium* by Thomas Tallis. This is a powerful piece for 40 voices, which, in the opinion of many, comes closest to the glory of heavenly music. What did the shepherds make of this, on top of all that they had already experienced? They were totally out of their comfort zone and this was something they could neither explain nor ever forget. What would they tell their families later that night? Would anyone believe them?

Having prepared for worship with these simple activities, everyone should now be ready to enter more fully into the singing of the carol.

*

IDEAS FOR EXPLORING THE CAROLS THROUGH CREATIVE PRAYER

Pebble pool prayers

Set up a pebble pool at the front of the worship space. For this, you will need a large shallow bowl, some large flat pebbles, one or two lengths of soft blue fabric, a large basket of small pebbles, some packs of confetti stars and a container in which to place the (loose) stars.

Fill the bowl with water and place the large pebbles in the bottom. Set the pool on a base of blue fabric. You will also need a large basket of smaller pebbles, enough for each person present. Read the words of Psalm 8 (see below), then invite people to take a small pebble out of the basket and place it in the water of the pebble pool. The small pebbles represent the things each one of us has thought, said or done that have caused us to turn away from Jesus' love. Invite people to think about those things as they slip their pebble into the pool.

Have the melody of the carol playing quietly in the background as people come up to place their pebbles in the pool.

Our Lord and Ruler, your name is wonderful everywhere on earth! You let your glory be seen in the heavens above. With praises from children and from tiny infants, you have built a fortress. It makes your enemies silent, and all who turn against you are left speechless. I often think of the heavens your hands have made, and of the moon and stars you put in place. Then I ask, 'Why do you care about us humans? Why are you concerned for us weaklings?' You made us a little lower than you yourself, and you have crowned us with glory and honour. You let us rule everything your hands have made. And you put all of it under our power—the sheep and the cattle, and every wild animal, the birds in the sky, the fish in the sea, and all ocean creatures. Our Lord and Ruler, your name is wonderful everywhere on earth!

PSALM 8

When everyone has placed their pebbles in the pool, invite them to cast a few confetti stars upon the water. Watch how the stars float on the surface of the water, while the pebbles sink to the bottom of the pool. The stars represent the promise of God that we are part of his family and that he will be with us always, covering our wrongdoings with his sacrificial love and fitting us for heaven and the promise of eternity.

Star prayers

Have a large cut-out of a five-pointed star. Colour each point as suggested below. Each of the five points represents a different topic for prayer, as follows:

- First point (blue): Prayers for our world
- Second point (red): Prayers for our country
- Third point (green): Prayers for our community
- Fourth point (yellow): Prayers for our family and friends
- Fifth point (pink): Prayers for ourselves

Hold the star so that everyone can see it. Ask five volunteers to take turns in holding the star, each by a different point. As each point is chosen, pray for that particular topic.

GOD REST YOU MERRY, GENTLEMEN

Praying together

Write the following three headings on three large sheets of card and display them at the front of the worship space.

- God's light…
- God's promise…
- God's peace…

Provide Post-it notes and a pen in the pews or seats for each member of the congregation. Invite everyone to write short prayers or reflections, or draw something, on separate Post-it notes for each of the three headings. (Younger members of the congregation may need adult help.) Let everyone know that their prayers or reflections may be read out. Play some gentle Christmas music while the reflection is in progress.

Giving time and space, invite everyone to place their Post-it notes on the sheets of card under the relevant heading. When everyone is finished, prayerfully read out the Post-it note reflections under each heading to create a corporate prayer of supplication, thanksgiving and praise. Be sure to include everyone's contribution or, if time is short, choose just a few from each heading.

GOOD KING WENCESLAS

Prayers in a nutshell

A Christmas tradition from the Czech Republic provides the possibility of a symbolic prayer activity. As part of Christmas celebrations, walnuts are cracked open and the half-shells used to make little boats that are floated on water. You will need to prepare beforehand enough half walnut shells to be distributed among the congregation. Each shell becomes the receptacle for the prayers, wishes and hopes of those holding them.

Place a large bowl of water at the front of the worship space and invite people to come up and float their walnut shells as an offering of prayer. The focus for their prayers should be the theme of this carol— that is, the needs of those who live in poverty around the world. As the shells are placed on the water, a leader should name situations for which the congregation has particular concerns and, especially at this time, the work of BibleLands and the people in the many projects it supports. (See www.biblelands.org.uk for more information.)

In the Czech tradition, the shells contain small candles. To simulate this safely, place a few ready-lit floating candles on the water. People should bring up their walnut prayers while some music is quietly played, and then everyone should say the following prayer together.

Lord Jesus Christ, you gave up your riches and became poor so that we could become rich. Hear our prayers for all those who are poor and needy in our world. Help them to stay afloat and discover the wind of your Spirit moving them into new places of grace and mercy. Bring the light of your love into their lives and into the lives of all those who seek to help them. Amen

HARK! THE HERALD-ANGELS SING

Light prayers

Light tealight candles in a sand tray for people, places or situations that are dark.

Sun of righteousness prayers

Draw a rising sun on a large sheet of card or paper. Give each person a triangular piece of yellow, white or orange card and ask them to choose a phrase or word from the carol to inspire a prayer. You might suggest 'peace on earth' and a prayer for a country at war, or 'healing in his wings' and a prayer for someone who is ill. They can write or draw the prayer on their triangle and come and place it on the rising sun. Someone could glue on the triangles with a glue stick during the service so that you have a prayer display to see at the end.

O COME, ALL YE FAITHFUL

You invite us to come

You could use the following prayer before or after the singing of the carol.

Lord, you never force us to believe in you.
You don't make us praise you.
You won't command us to love you.
But instead, you invite us to come.

Lord, you don't deliberately wait out of sight.
You don't always hide and leave us guessing.
You don't just hope we'll notice you.
But instead, you invite us to come.

Lord, you took such a great risk for us.
You let go of so much.
You made the first move.
Lord, you invite us to come.

Lord, you opened the door first.
You made it all possible.
You cleared the way between us.
Lord, you invite us to come.

Lord, you long for our coming.
You came to meet our longing.
You loved us first.
Lord, you invite us to come.

The invitation

Jesus invites us to follow him. He began his work with the invitation 'come' to the disciples. He ends his ministry with the words 'go'. But the inbetween part is down to us. Will we accept his invitation? Here is a simple version of the carol that emphasizes the invitation.

> *Jesus is here—come, filled with joy*
> *Jesus is God—come, filled with awe*
> *Jesus is born—come, filled with song*
> *Jesus will rescue—come and see*

This carol is a great invitation to worship, but it also opens up other sorts of invitations—invitations to imagine what it would be like from the different perspectives in the carol. Perhaps the following questions will start a discussion and inspire some creative work on the carol, which could be used in the service.

- **Verse 1**: What might it feel like to be invited to see God? What feelings are going on inside? How can you describe the joy and anticipation? Can you measure the pride and fear?
- **Verse 2**: What might it have felt like for God to become as small as a baby? What does it mean to go from being all-powerful to being helpless? What is it like, leaving the place where all light comes from to being lit up by just a star in a dark stable?
- **Verse 3**: What might heaven make of all this? Just what is God up to? Why does he care so much for the people of earth? What sort of songs do angels sing?

- **Verse 4**: What would you say to the baby? How would you show honour and respect? How can we give glory to Jesus? What evidence of God's presence is there in this tiny baby?

O LITTLE TOWN OF BETHLEHEM

Abide with us

This carol brings together three phrases that could become a focus for a creative time of prayer during the service. The three phrases are 'the dark streets', 'this world of sin' and 'the hopes and fears of all the years'. The streets could become the local streets in your neighbourhood for which you want to pray. The world is a prompt for the global issues that will be in the headlines at this time. The hopes and fears represent the longings of many people at Christmas who hope for peace and a new start, especially if it has been a difficult year.

In fact, the carol ends on a prayer: 'O come to us, abide with us, our Lord Emmanuel.' This final prayer can become a response for the congregation following each of the following sections.

Light shining in the dark streets

Invite the congregation to call out the names of the roads and streets in their area, and also include any others named by visitors at the service. After a pause, collect the prayers together with the following words:

Leader:　Lord, we ask that the everlasting light of Jesus may shine in our streets this Christmas.

All:　O come to us, abide with us, our Lord Emmanuel.

Light shining in the world of sin

Invite the congregation to call out places in the world that are suffering and in the headlines at this time. After a pause, collect the prayers together with the following words:

Leader: Lord, we ask that the everlasting light of Jesus may shine into these places this Christmas.

All: O come to us, abide with us, our Lord Emmanuel.

Lght shining into our own lives

Invite the congregation, in a moment of silence, to lift up all that has gone on in the past year, and then to focus for a short while on their hopes for the coming year. After a pause, collect the prayers together with the following words:

Leader: Lord, we ask that the everlasting light of Jesus may shine into our hopes and fears this Christmas.

All: O come to us, abide with us, our Lord Emmanuel.

ONCE IN ROYAL DAVID'S CITY

Tissue paper pattern confession

This idea might work well in the confession part of the service. You will need to practise folding a circle of paper and ripping it so that it makes a snowflake pattern.

Show a perfect tissue paper circle, big enough for everyone to see. Say the words, 'He is our childhood's pattern' and then pray the following prayer.

Jesus, you were a baby and a child, just as we all are now or once were. You were a whole child, a healthy child, a full and perfect child. You never made wrong choices. You were full of love. You never set out to hurt people. You never did things that make God sad. You grew wise and strong and people loved you.

Take a second circle of tissue paper and fold it as you speak, ripping pieces out of it and crushing it so that it looks like a limp rag.

But we are damaged in so many ways as we grow up. Sometimes we make wrong choices. Sometimes other people rip away at our self-confidence. Sometimes we are weak. Sometimes we deliberately hurt other people. Sometimes we do things that we know will make you sad. We aren't perfect. We are ripped and torn and crumpled. We are sorry when we make a mess of things.

Unfold the tissue paper, which has turned into a snowflake pattern.

Thank you that you love us whatever we do or think or say. Thank you that you forgive us and give us a new start when we say sorry. Thank you that you can make us beautiful in a whole new way, every time we come back to you.

Tears and smiles

Explain that Christmas is a happy time for many people, but is also a sad time for many. Speak out the words from the carol, 'Jesus feels for our sadness'. Suggest countries, people or situations that need our prayer because the people there are sad today.

Jesus also shares our gladness. What happy situations, answers to prayer and causes for thanks can we praise him for?

SILENT NIGHT

Praying in the dark

Here is an idea for prayer based on two lines of the carol.

Silent night, holy night

Display pictures of the moon and stars.

• What can we say 'thank you' for about night time and quiet?

Thank you for the gift of silence. Thank you for the gift of night's darkness, for the moon and stars and all their beauty.

Display pictures of someone afraid at night, of bombs exploding during the night, of dark neighbourhoods.

• Who needs prayer at night?

We pray for those who are scared of the dark, for those for whom night time means bombs, gunshots and violence of war, for those whose nights are times of fear, and for those whose neighbourhoods are noisy or frightening.

Sleep in heavenly peace

Display pictures of snug beds, teddies, hot water bottles and other images of safety.

• What can we say thank you for, when we think about sleeping?

Thank you for the gift of sleep and dreams. Thank you for warm beds and soft pillows. Thank you for teddies and cuddly blankets and hot water bottles, for people who read us bedtime stories or sing to us. Thank you for a time to switch off from the cares of the day and to get energy for the next day.

Display pictures of someone crying, babies crying, adults awake at night time, streetchildren asleep in the open.

• Who needs prayer for sleep?

We pray for those who cannot sleep because they are sad,
For those who cannot sleep because of pain or illness,
For those who have to work shifts at night,
For those who suffer from nightmares,
For those with small children who are woken during the night,
For those who need more sleep because of illness or busyness,
For those who have nowhere safe to sleep, such as streetchildren in the cities of our world.

Written prayers

While the carol 'Silent night' is playing, display a picture of modern-day Bethlehem in all its wartorn precariousness. Invite everyone to write a prayer for peace on a Post-it note or a cut-out dove shape and to place the prayers around the crib scene.

Silent prayer time

Display a slideshow of pictures to inspire prayer, especially countries at war, families broken apart or broken friendships. Invite everyone to pray silently for situations that the pictures remind them of. It may be appropriate to have the carol melody playing in the background.

Prayers for peace

The dove is often seen as a symbol for peace, perhaps because of its role in the story of Noah's ark, perhaps because of its inherently gentle nature, or perhaps because Pablo Picasso painted one as the symbol for the International Peace Congress in 1949. The dove also features on Christmas cards, both as a symbol of peace and, perhaps, because of its resemblance to the angels: its colour, its wings, and its role as a messenger in the Noah story all link closely to traditional images of angels.

The crane is an Asian symbol of peace. Tell the story of Sadako Sasaki, who suffered directly from the effects of war.

In 1955, Sadako, a twelve-year-old Japanese girl, was diagnosed with leukaemia, having been exposed to nuclear radiation after the bombings of Hiroshima and Nagasaki. She heard that she would be granted a wish if she folded 1000 origami paper cranes. So she started folding the paper cranes, wishing for a well body in a world of peace. Although she sadly died before she had completed the thousand cranes, her efforts have inspired the foundation of an organization whose aim is to unite children of the world in an effort for peace.

Details of the story, instructions for folding cranes and a song to sing can be found on the Internet.

You could write prayers on squares of paper and make paper cranes out of these squares to display as mobiles.

THE FIRST NOWELL

Inside out

Here is a prayer that could be used before or after the singing of the carol.

You knew about the shepherds, working late at night,
You knew about the travellers following the light,
You know about outsiders, who feel they don't belong,

You know about the stranger, who speaks another tongue,
You know about the exile, who is forced to leave his home,
You know about the foreigner, who feels so much alone,
You know about the poor, whom nobody will know,
You know about the puzzled, who feel they've far to go.
You bring them close in Jesus, each specially loved by him,
You turn all things inside out and bring outsiders in.

WE THREE KINGS

Our spiritual journey

The wise men were on a journey of discovery. In a similar way today, as Christians, we are on a spiritual journey as we travel onwards in life, closer and closer to Jesus. Sometimes the journey is fun and sometimes it is hard. We're all at different places on the journey.

Make space for everyone to take some time to pray for each other, for the worldwide family of believers and for themselves. The prayer journey below follows the journey of the wise men as depicted in the carol—through field and fountain, moor and mountain, following yonder star.

If you prefer to sit still, you may like to use the *Bethlehem Carol Sheet* to help prompt your prayers. If you prefer to move around, set up five prayer stations, one for each of the five places to visit. Write the different prayer prompts on card and place them at the appropriate stations. Invite everyone to spend as much or as little time at each prayer station as they need. Be aware that some people may need help to light candles. Play some quiet music during the prayer time and, to close, draw the prayers together with a song.

Field

Place some blades of grass next to a tray of sand, with the following words from Psalm 23.

You let me rest in fields of green grass.
PSALM 23:2A

Prayer prompt: Take a moment to thank God for rest and refreshment at this holiday time. Pray for those who have to work or are desperately tired and need a break. Place a blade of green grass on the sand tray as a sign of your prayer.

Fountain

Provide a bowl of water and floating candles with a means of lighting them, and the following words from Isaiah.

When you cross deep rivers, I will be with you, and you won't drown.
ISAIAH 43:2

Prayer prompt: Light a candle and float it on the water. Pray for someone, a country or a group of people in deep water at the moment.

Moor

Place some rough pieces of wood with some small pieces of sandpaper and the following words, again from the book of Isaiah.

'Clear a path in the desert! Make a straight road for the Lord our God… Level the rough and rugged ground. Then the glory of the Lord will appear for all to see!'
ISAIAH 40:3–5

Prayer prompt: Feel a piece of wood. Ask God to show you parts of your life that are rough and unfinished. Ask God to change you to be more like Jesus so that people will see him in your life. Gently sand down the wood as you pray.

Mountain

Provide a picture of a mountain on which people can write (or Post-it notes that they can write on and stick to the picture) and the following Bible verse.

The Lord gives strength to those who are weary. Even young people get tired, then stumble and fall. But those who trust in the Lord will find new strength. They will be strong like eagles soaring upward on wings; they will walk and run without getting tired.
ISAIAH 40:29–31

Prayer prompt: Pray for anyone known to you personally or in the news who is on an uphill journey at the moment. Write or draw your prayer for them on the picture of the mountain, in the spot where you or they seem to be at the moment.

Following yonder star

Provide a large expanse of dark cloth, silver foil stars and the following Bible passage.

Their road is dark and rough, but I will give them light to keep them from stumbling.
ISAIAH 42:16

Prayer prompt: Pick up some stars. Who are your guiding lights? Thank God for the light in your life. Place the stars in the night sky.

WHILE SHEPHERDS WATCHED

The good news of Jesus

The moods and story of this carol could inspire some intercessory prayer. Use the repeated line for the whole congregation and have different leaders, including children, speak the biddings.

Leader 1: Let us pray for those whose work takes them far from home.

All: Thank you that the good news of Jesus is for everyone.

Leader 2: Let us pray for those who are frightened and worried tonight.

All: Thank you that the good news of Jesus is for everyone.

Leader 3: Let us pray for those waiting for a promise to be kept.

All: Thank you that the good news of Jesus is for everyone.

Leader 4: Let us pray for those expecting a baby soon.

All: Thank you that the good news of Jesus is for everyone.

Leader 5: Let us pray for any who are surprised by the way things have turned out for them.

All: Thank you that the good news of Jesus is for everyone.

Leader 6: Let us pray for those who work hard for peace on earth.

All: Thank you that the good news of Jesus is for everyone.

Leader 7: Let us pray for those who don't feel joy-filled this Christmas.

All: Thank you that the good news of Jesus is for everyone.

Glory to you, heavenly Father

Here is a prayer linked to a meditation on this carol by Gordon Giles in his book *O Come, Emmanuel* (BRF, 2005).

Glory to you, heavenly Father,
For in Christ you have cast away our fear
And, by your angels,
Have brought us a hope of good will among all nations.
Keep watch over us, the sheep of your pasture,
And lead us into all peace,
Until that day when, with angels and archangels,
We will sing your praises in the highest heaven,
Where you reign,
With the Spirit and the Son,
Jesus Christ our Lord.
Amen

＊

IDEAS FOR UNDER-FIVES

AWAY IN A MANGER

In the poem below, use hand actions to describe the shape for the words in bold. For example:

- **Stable:** Hold up both hands facing each other (palms inward) and then bend the fingers to join in the middle to create a shelter.
- **Star:** With both hands, open and close the fingers several times in a twinkling gesture.
- **Baby:** Rock an imaginary baby in your arms.
- **Jesus:** Touch the palm of each hand with the index finger of the opposite hand (the sign for Jesus in British Sign Language).

*This is the **stable** where Jesus will lie.*
*This is the **star** that appeared in the sky.*
*This is the **baby** asleep on the hay.*
***Jesus** was born on the first Christmas Day.*

Praying hands

This activity is linked to the suggestion that the first two lines of verse 3 could be a prayer for young children to learn.

In preparation, make a pair of praying hands for each child by drawing around a hand on folded card, placing the edge of the hand against the fold of the card. Cut through both pieces of card and open out. Make a label on which is printed the two-line prayer. Ask the children to stick a picture of Jesus in the manger on the inside of one hand, and the prayer label on the inside of the other hand.

A Christmas tree decoration

In preparation, draw a simple outline picture of Jesus in a manger and reproduce it on to thin card. Cut around the outline. Punch a hole for a hanging thread. Either ask the children to colour in the picture or have pre-cut textured pieces for them to stick on to the picture—for example, wood effect paper for the crib, raffia for straw, vivelle or felt for the baby shape. Place a thread through the hole and tie the ends in a secure knot.

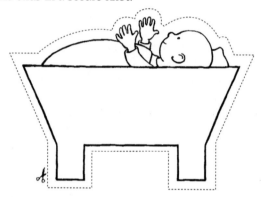

GOD REST YOU MERRY, GENTLEMEN

Chorus only!

Teach children the chorus so that they can join in with that part of the carol. Prearrange a signal that children can look out for, so that they will know when to come in.

Chime along

Use simple percussion instruments to accompany the chorus. Have someone to take the role of conductor to bring the children in at the right moment.

Pass it on

One theme in the carol is about passing on good news. Play a game in small groups where an adult passes on some good news to the first child by whispering it in their ear. The child passes the news on to the next child in the same way. You could play this game sitting in a line or in a circle.

GOOD KING WENCESLAS

Simplifying the story

The story of this carol can be simplified for an under-fives group. The following version is set to the melody of 'I saw three ships come sailing by'. Each verse has an accompanying action that the children can learn to help carry the meaning of the story.

Verse 1

The children shade their eyes with one hand and scan the horizon.

The king looked at the snow so deep
On Boxing Day, on Boxing Day.
The king looked at the snow so deep
On Boxing Day, in the morning.

Verse 2

The children mime picking up sticks.

He saw a poor man gathering sticks
To make a fire, to make a fire.
He saw a poor man gathering sticks
To keep him warm on that morning.

Verse 3

The children point far away in the distance.

'He lives right at the forest edge,'
His servant said, his servant said.
'He lives right at the forest edge,
Just beside the mountain.'

Verse 4

The children mime packing a parcel.

The king collected food and drink
To take to him, to take to him.
The king collected food and drink,
To help that man in the morning.

Verse 5

The children mime trudging through the snow.

The servant and the king set out
Through deepest snow, through deepest snow.
The servant and the king set out
With Christmas gifts that morning.

Verse 6

The children mime a giving action with both hands.

The king, like Jesus, helped the poor.
He showed kindness, he showed kindness.
Help us, like Jesus, care for all
And follow him this Christmas.

Dress the ted

Invite young children to dress a teddy in warm clothes, ready to go out in the snow. Give each child a cut-out of a teddy figure, with cut-outs of a coat, a scarf, a hat and boots. Stick the clothes and boots on the teddy.

Following footsteps

Cut out adult-sized footprints from paper and place them on the floor as if treading a path. Fasten them to the floor so they do not slip. Invite the children to follow the same pathway by treading in the same footmarks.

HARK! THE HERALD-ANGELS SING

Angels all

Teach children the chorus of the carol. Prearrange a signal that the children watch for (this could be an angel picture) so that they know when to come in.

Hanging angel

Make a simple angel. In preparation, for each child you will need a triangular shape for the body (round off the corners) about 13cm long and 10.5cm at the widest point, a circle of white card for the head, about 5.5cm diameter, one quarter of a doily for each wing, ribbon for the halo and some hanging thread.

Punch a hole in the top of the circle for the hanging thread. Using small glue sticks, help the children to stick the card circle on top of the body shape, attach the wings to the back of the body shape and stick ribbon across the top of the card circle for the halo.

Thread a length of ribbon through the hole in the top of the circle and tie it to make a loop so that the angel can be hung on a Christmas tree.

For more detailed instructions, see the 'Early Years' section of the 'Ideas' part of www.barnabasinchurches.org.uk.

Angel chains

Make an angel chain. For each child you will need half of a piece of A4 paper, cut lengthwise. Fold the paper, concertina style, into four. Draw a simple angel shape on the top piece, making sure that the wings come to the folds. Cut around the angel shape, being careful to keep the pieces attached at the folds. Open out the chain.

You could provide materials to embellish the angel chain—for example, crayons or glitter. Encourage the children to hold the chain up (a hand on either end) when they sing the chorus.

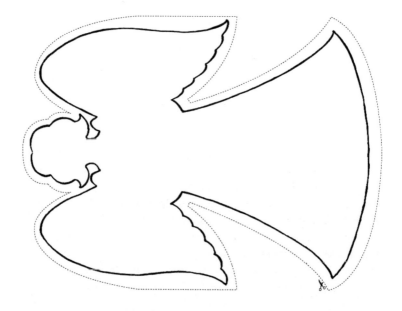

O COME, ALL YE FAITHFUL

Hands up for Jesus

Teach the chorus of this carol to your children with some simple actions.

- Hands beckoning towards you for 'come'
- Hands raised high, or in prayer, for 'adore'
- Hands holding an imaginary baby for 'Christ the Lord'

The children could use percussion instruments to accompany the chorus. A 'conductor' could encourage them to start softly, but get louder each time.

Nativity tableaux

Ask a leader to read the verses of the carol and, at the appropriate moment, move wooden or soft toy versions of the nativity figures to form a central display. For example, the shepherds come in slowly for verse 1 and keep moving during the other verses too; Mary, Joseph and the baby come in for verse 2; angels are brought in for verse 3. The figures have all arrived and taken their places for the last verse. For a more modern version of the verses, see page 131.

Welcome to Bethlehem

Make a communal poster. This carol invites us all to Bethlehem to see Jesus. Place a silhouette picture of Jesus in the manger in the middle of a large sheet of paper. Give everyone a circle of paper and invite them to draw a picture of themselves with eyes, mouth and hair. Stick the faces around the manger.

Footsteps to Bethlehem

Cut out a strip of paper to represent a winding roadway. Cut out an outline of a building to represent the stable and stick pictures of Mary, Joseph and Jesus inside. Ask parents and carers to draw around their children's feet on paper and then cut out the outlines. If practical, the children could decorate their foot cut-outs with paper shapes, wools, textured materials and so on. Stick the feet on to the roadway.

Bethlehem flags

Make a flag from paper. Draw a picture of Jesus in the manger on the flag and fasten the flag to a stout straw. Encourage children to wave the flags when they sing the chorus.

O LITTLE TOWN OF BETHLEHEM

Bethlehem stars

Make a poster for the carol. Draw or attach a silhouette outline of a simple building towards the bottom of a large sheet of paper. Using large-sized print, add the message across the top of the poster: 'O morning stars, together proclaim the holy birth'. Inside the building silhouette, place outlines of Mary and Joseph, and Jesus in a manger. You could use a gold colour for Jesus. Give everyone a star and invite them to attach their star to the poster, above the building.

Morning stars

This idea also relates to the lines from the second verse: 'O morning stars, together, proclaim the holy birth'. Prepare for each child a star shape made from stiff card, a picture of Jesus in the manger and a length of ribbon for a hanging thread.

Punch a hole near the top of one of the points of the star. Make available some glue sticks and some glitter. Invite the children to stick the picture of Jesus in the middle of the star, and decorate the surrounding part of the star by using the glue stick to make trails of glue and then sprinkling on the glitter. A practical tip is to put the glitter in a tray and provide spoons for sprinkling it. Shake the surplus glitter back into the tray.

Thread the ribbon through the holes and tie the ends together. Suggest that this could be the star for the top of a Christmas tree.

Everlasting light

This idea relates to the line in the first verse that refers to Jesus as 'the everlasting light'. For each child you will need a picture of Jesus as a baby in the manger, reproduced on to an A4 acetate sheet. Try to use a picture with a bold black outline. (If you photocopy the pictures, make sure that you copy them on to photocopiable acetate sheets. If you use marker pens, make sure that they contain permanent ink.) If you wish, you could also make a card frame for each child. You will also need torn pieces of tissue paper and glue sticks.

Glue pieces of tissue to the reverse side of the acetate picture. Encourage children to cover the whole piece. Fasten a frame around the edge, and punch two holes in the top of the picture for a hanging thread. When hung on a window, the light will shine through and give a 'stained glass' effect.

ONCE IN ROYAL DAVID'S CITY

Turn-around faces

Developing further the 'tears and smiles' idea, children could make turn-around faces. Each child will need two circles of paper for faces, with collage materials to make eyes and hair. They will also need two curved pieces for the mouth, one to be stuck on as a smiley mouth and one as a sad mouth. Stick the two faces together, back to back, sandwiching a straw between the two faces at the bottom.

There may be an opportunity to talk to the children about what makes them sad and what makes them happy. Children can look at the sad face when thinking about Jesus sharing in our sadness, and then turn it round to look at the happy face when thinking about Jesus sharing in our joy.

And he leads his children on

Make a chain of people going to Jesus. Give each parent and carer a sheet of A4 paper, a pencil and a pair of child-safe scissors. Ask the adults to help the children to fold the paper concertina-style and then draw the shape of a person on the top layer, making sure the arms come to the folds. They then need to cut around the outline, being careful to leave the joins at the edges intact. Provide some glue sticks and invite everyone to stick their chains on to a poster, pointing towards a picture of Jesus. In large letters, write a message for the poster: 'And he leads his children on'.

Stable scene

The first two verses of the carol create a picture of the stable as Jesus' place of birth. Make available some construction sets (for example, Duplo), wooden blocks and some appropriate stable animals. In small groups, encourage the children to build a stable and create the stable scene.

This activity will work better if there is an adult with each group to help keep the children focused on the task.

SILENT NIGHT

Night time stories

Read a story such as *The owl who was afraid of the dark* (Jill Tomlinson, Egmont Children's Books), or *Can't you sleep, little bear?* (Martin Waddell and Barbara Firth, Walker Books).

Candlelit carol

People often like to sing this carol by candlelight. Invite the children to make imitation candles. For each child you will need a cardboard tube (for example, the inside of a kitchen roll), white paper and a flame shape made from orange or yellow card. Stick the white paper around the cardboard tube and attach the flame to the side at the top of the tube so that it stands above the tube.

THE FIRST NOWELL

It's a birthday!

Pick up on the idea of choosing people to come to a party. Who would you invite to a party? God invites unexpected guests—the people no one likes and who aren't popular. God invites unexpected visitors—the people no one understands (remember, the wise men would have spoken a different language) and who are unfamiliar. These guests were also tired guests (perhaps the shepherds were yawning!) and weary guests (the wise men must have arrived tired and footsore after their long journey).

> *It's a birthday, a birthday,*
> *Who must we invite?*
> *Neighbours, friends and family,*

That surely must be right.
But 'No, not these,' says God.
'I've someone else in mind—
The outsider and unrecognized,
The ones life leaves behind.
The foreigners and nobodies,
They'll be first to see
The baby born as God on earth,
And join in praise to me.'
Now I see that no one is
An outsider to our Lord.
Inside God's love, there's room for all:
No one is ignored.

Nowell mimes

Here are some simple actions and sounds to go with the key points in the story.

- Baby in arms for 'Born is the king…'
- Bell ringing for 'Nowell'
- Being asleep for the shepherds
- Bobbing up and down on camels for the wise men
- Kneeling with gifts when the wise men arrive
- Hands in the air and then hands on heart as everyone sings praise about the salvation Jesus brings

Beforehand, play some sleeping games and waiting games and mime the various actions in preparation.

Finger rhyme

Bring hands together from wide apart and link them up as a cage. Turn the cage inside out and wiggle fingers. Use the following rhyme:

Jesus brings outsiders in
Jesus turns things inside out

Good news flags

The carol speaks of the 'good news' of Jesus' birth being given to the shepherds and then to the wise men. We, too, can bring the good news of Jesus' birth to other people.

Make a flag from paper. Stick on a picture of Jesus in the manger, and fasten the flag to a stout straw. Encourage children to wave the flags as a way of telling other people about the good news of Jesus' birth.

WE THREE KINGS

Christmas tree stars

Make stars to hang on the children's Christmas trees.

Follow my leader

Mime the 'story' in the carol. Have an adult hold the star on a long garden cane. Dress up three older children as wise men. The younger children follow on and play a game similar to 'follow my leader'. The group move around the worship space, the wise men picking up on actions in the carol and the children copying.

Star turns

Teach children the chorus of the carol. Prearrange a signal that the children watch for (this could be a star) so that they know when to come in.

WHILE SHEPHERDS WATCHED

Stepping into the story

The rhythm and rhyme of this popular carol has meant that at least some of its words are quite easily picked up, even by very young children—perhaps particularly the words of verses 1, 2 and 6. With the younger children, it would make sense to focus on just these verses (or perhaps only two of them) and, to help the words sink in, to link them to some simple mime actions.

Start with children sitting on the ground and then suddenly standing up as they sing verse 1. Next, the children should become scared and look at each other in bewilderment as the angel's words of verse 2 are sung. Then they should hold their hands up high for the 'all glory' of verse 6, pointing up for the first line and down to the earth for the second. Finally, a 'thumbs up' should be held high and brought low for lines three and four, ending with both hands thumbs up and circling around each other as a visual demonstration of 'begin and never cease'.

Shepherds watching

Here's a simple one-verse version of the carol to the melody of 'London's burning', to use with younger children.

Shepherds watching, shepherds watching,
Angels singing, angels singing,
News, news; news, news,
Peace on earth now; peace on earth now.

Flocks by night

Invite the children to make a cut-out of a sheep. For each child, fold a piece of white A5 paper in half. With the fold at the top, draw and cut out a sheep shape, cutting through both layers. Take care to leave a significant part of the fold at the top intact. Attach small pieces of cotton wool to the sheep's body.

*

BIBLIOGRAPHY

GENERAL BOOKS

Gordon Giles, *O Come, Emmanuel*, BRF, 2005.

Thomas Hardy, *Under the Greenwood Tree*, Oxford World's Classics, OUP, 1985.

Jean Hatton, *The Light Bearers*, Monarch Books, 2003. (Traces the history of BibleLands from its beginnings in 1854 to the present day.)

John McCarthy and Jill Morrell, *Some Other Rainbow*, Bantam Press, 1993.

POETRY

David Adam, *The Edge of Glory: Prayers in the Celtic Tradition*, Triangle, 1985.

Mary Batchelor (ed.), *The Lion Christian Poetry Collection*, Lion Hudson plc, 1995.

T.S. Eliot, *Selected Poems*, Faber, 1956.

Sidney Godolphin (1610–93), in Helen Gardner (ed.), *The New Oxford Book of English Verse, 1250–1950*, OUP, 1972.

Thomas Hardy, *The Illustrated Poets*, Aurum Press Ltd, 1990.

Kate McIlhagga, 'Christmastide' from *The Green Heart of the Snowdrop*, Wild Goose Publications, 2004

Gerard Manley Hopkins, *Oxford Poetry Library*, OUP, 1995.

'The Eve of St Agnes' by John Keats (1795–1821). *Everyman Anthology (Volume 4)* published by J.M. Dent (Orion Publishing Group), 1996. Originally published in 1820 in London under the title of *Lamia, Isabella, The Eve of St Agnes and Other Poems*

Isaac Watts, 'Miracles at the Birth of Christ', in Gardner (ed.), *The New Oxford Book of English Verse, 1250–1950*

DRAMA

Peter Shaw, *All-Age Sketches for the Christian Year*, Barnabas, 2006.

MUSIC

Bertram L. Barnaby, *In Concert Sing: Hymns and Their Verse*, Canterbury Press, 1996.

Alan Dunstan, *The Use of Hymns*, Kevin Mayhew, 1996.

John Harper, *Forms and Orders of Western Liturgy from 10th to the 18th Century*, OUP, 1991.

Erik Routley, *The Musical Wesleys*, Herbert Jenkins, 1968.

Erik Routley (ed.), *University Carol Book*, Freeman, 1961.

Percy Scholes (ed.), *Concise Oxford Dictionary of Music*, OUP, 2004.

R. Vaughan Williams (ed.), *English Hymnal*, OUP, 1933.

R. Vaughan Williams (ed.), *Oxford Book of Carols*, OUP, 1964.

*

BIBLE INDEX